KGGM
CBS

SHOES

D0792960

OYD BRIDGES   JOHN IRELAND
"LITTLE BIG HORN"
SADDLER-PEP CHAMPIONSHIP BOUT

Albuquerque
in Our Time
30 Voices, 300 Years

by Debra Hughes

Museum of New Mexico Press Santa Fe

Project editor: Mary Wachs
Design and Production: David Skolkin
Manuscript editing: Peg Goldstein/Neatnik Editorial
Manufactured in U.S.A.
10 9 8 7 6 5 4 3 2 1

ISBN 0-89013-481-2 (pbk)

Museum of New Mexico Press
Post Office Box 2087
Santa Fe, New Mexico 87504

Photos front cover: (clockwise from top) Central and First, 1925, photo by William H. Cobb. Courtesy Ward Hicks Collection, Albuquerque Museum PA 1982.180.361; pg. 27 bottom; pg 125; pg 23 bottom; Chester T. French Boys Choir, courtesy Albuquerque Museum PA 1978.151.360; (left) pg. 93, (right) pg. 81; pg. 24.

Photo back cover: Sunshine Theatre, 1940s, by Jerry Allred, courtesy Albuquerque Museum, PA 1982.181.200.

Photos pg. 1: (inset) Bystander at transatlantic balloon-crossing parade, 1978. Courtesy Patty Anderson. (Background) Central Avenue looking west at corner of First and Central, 1950, Courtesy Albuquerque National Bank, Albuquerque Progress Collection.

Pg. 2-3: New Mexico State Fair parade, 1951, Eddy County Mounted Posse marches east. Photo by Rexx Curtis, Donated by Charlie Frelund, Courtesy Albuquerque Museum PA 1999.5.957.

Contents

I grew up in Albuquerque in the 1950s and 1960s, went away to college, came back, left and returned again, and when my children were small moved north to Santa Fe. That was fifteen years ago. Over the course of those fifteen years, although I lived only sixty miles north, the everyday sense of Albuquerque faded, an impediment to researching and writing this book, I feared. When the research phase began, I spent the first week driving the streets of the city. I drove from one end of Central Avenue to the other and back down again. On Rio Grande Boulevard I did the same, as well as on San Mateo, Indian School Road, Academy, and Coors Boulevard. After two or three tanks of gas, I had covered a good deal of Albuquerque's road grid. I got lost, took my time, and slowly the impediment I had felt earlier dissolved. I knew this place. Yes, the city had changed, but so had I—and I liked the freshness. I stopped for a meal at Duran's Pharmacy. The magazine rack seemed bigger, the lotion and soap section more expansive, but the smell of their chile—unmistaken

Preface

comfort. Soon enough, after time spent in libraries, bookstores, gas stations, restaurants, museums, and the university, the city's rhythm took hold in its mixed syncopated beat, a combination of Latin, cowboy, Benny Goodman, and eighties rock. The floodgates opened: childhood, adolescence, early motherhood. The memories would not stop.

Sunshine in the Night
In the 1940s, the Sunshine Theatre and the KiMo Theatre were the hotspots of town. Photograph by Jerry Allred from the Ward Hicks collection. Courtesy Albuquerque Museum. PA1982.181.200.

I am honored to have shared these memories and moments of reflection with everyone included in this book. While the process of interviewing and developing these pieces took six months, my connections with many of these people span decades. Many are old friends and acquaintances. Casey and Blair Darnell taught me to ride and care for a horse as a youngster, and their daughter Kris and I went to school together. Lisa Madsen Maurer and I played on the North Valley ditches. Patty Anderson's daughter Stephanie and I attended the same high school, and my family and I watched as their hot-air balloons first floated above our home and scared our horses into a frenzy. The Simmses and my family became longtime friends. Anthony Anella and I circulated with the same group while attending Valley High School. There were Al Hurricane concerts at the Civic Auditorium and his ads all over the radio airwaves. I worked as a fledgling journalist when Conroy Chino and Miguel Gandert were beginning their careers in broadcast news. Through the years, I bought jeans and cowboy boots from Cooper's Western Warehouse—Roberta Cooper Ramo's family-owned store—and enjoyed barbecue at Powdrell's. I've eaten my fair share of hot chile enchiladas at Michael Gonzales's Barelas Coffee House, too. Rubén Cobos still lives on the street where I spent my infancy and schoolgirl years, a nice coincidence though we never met. Tony Hillerman spoke at one of my writing workshops, and Ray Powell became a veterinarian when my father, Clint Hughes, had a small-animal medical practice. I have recently met others in the book through introduction, a bit of legwork, or pure luck. Albuquerque—we all agreed we could go on about it for hours.

Within these pages, individuals respond to my request to examine a time, place, or event, or a combination of the three, that best speaks to what life was or is like in this city. Because each person delivered a story in a distinct and strong way, I chose to present these narratives in the first person, so that readers can "hear" the voices on the page as they were spoken to me during interviews. I selected people who have spent a good deal of their lives in Albuquerque. There are public figures, some of whom helped shape the city in its dramatic growth after World War II; there are civil servants, owners of popular restaurants and gathering places, neighborhood leaders, artists, an architect, cultural preservationists, and people who work to protect the city's environment and open space. There are voices from the city's horse and agricultural communities; a scientist talks about global technology stemming from the city, a retired physician reflects on the medical field of days past, and a photographer shares the mysteries that have come before his lens. In my piece on childhood in Albuquerque, I have taken the creative liberty to change a few names and details, as the fantasies of a child sometimes will. Together, these stories represent the diverse heart of Albuquerque and a little bit of its soul.

Coined a "nuts and bolts" kind of place, Albuquerque has its practical side, not necessarily a pretty one. As the state's largest city, it sprawls with highways and fast traffic. Chain stores and restaurants dominate the landscape, with the sterile effect of sameness that makes Albuquerque like every other American city of half a million. But under the veneer, Albuquerque's character stubbornly thrives: A person can go to a Wendy's or McDonald's or Burger King and order green chile added to a sandwich. The city celebrates a mix of architectural extremes, from low adobe buildings with flat roofs—a style used by native Pueblo Indians—to the high-tech, military-style, glass and metal buildings connected with Sandia National Laboratories and Kirtland Air Force Base. Tony Hillerman said in his interview that when it came time to become serious about writing, Albuquerque gave him the grounding to write novels, essays, and nonfiction books. "I'm a Harry Truman kind of guy," he said, who prefers the simple lifestyle to the glamorous. Others echoed Hillerman's sentiment. Still others told stories of conflict, beauty, and surprise. All these stories are presented in respect to a vital city at an important juncture: its three hundredth year of recorded history, reason enough for celebration and reflection.

A very special thank you goes to Anna Gallegos, director of the Museum of New Mexico Press, for visualizing this collection of memoirs, and to Mary Wachs, Editorial Director, who shared her foresight and twists of humor tirelessly throughout the book's progress. I send my gratitude to Martha Day, former development director of KNME-TV, for her enthusiasm and ideas. Also, I thank the following people for their patient, friendly support: Bob Taichert, a dear friend and longtime New Mexican; Melissa Mann, Dick Ruddy, and Morris Rippel of the Albuquerque Museum Photo-Archive Department; Ann Carson, president of the Albuquerque Conservation Association; Mary Davis, former preservation planner for Albuquerque and author of *Shining River, Precious Land* (Albuquerque Museum 1986, 1996); Melanie LaBorwit, curator of education, and Marilee Nason, collections curator, with the Anderson-Abruzzo Albuquerque International Balloon Museum; Charlotte Balcomb Lane,

Acknowledgments

granddaughter of early Albuquerque writer Ross Calvin and columnist for the *Albuquerque Journal*; John German of Sandia National Laboratories; Ana Baca of Bueno Foods; and Mo Palmer, former director of photo archives at the Albuquerque Museum and self-described pop-culture historian.

Especially, I thank my mother and father, Jo and Clint Hughes, for having planted roots in such a mysterious and wonderful place. To my sons, Merritt and Austin, who know and carry New Mexico in their souls, and to Gary, thank you.

Public Art

A huge arrow pierces the ground at Sproul's Indian Plaza at the corner of Carlisle and Indian School Road. Photograph by Steve Donahue. Courtesy Albuquerque Museum. PA1999.44.21.

No one has pinned down the exact date when men and women arrived in the Middle Rio Grande Valley, where Albuquerque now sits. But evidence of carved stone shows that as early as 9500 to 9000 B.C. humans hunted the huge imperial mammoth here. Since then, varying cultures have moved through the area, some staying only long enough to build fire pits and lodges of animal skins and poles, others settling in to gather seeds and plants and to hunt small animals. We call this latter group the Desert culture. They transitioned into the Basket Maker culture, a group that raised crops and made finely woven baskets. At first they lived in pit houses, then advanced to aboveground homes made of adobe or stone. Theirs was the beginning of today's Pueblo Indian culture.

Pueblo villages began to appear north and south of Albuquerque after A.D. 1300. Kuaua (now Coronado State Monument) was one such pueblo. It encompassed twelve hun-

Introduction

dred rooms, two plazas, and six kivas—all built over a span of three hundred years before 1600. After this date, the people of Kuaua left their village and moved five miles south to what is now Sandia Pueblo.

Although the Pueblo people preferred a quiet existence, life in the pueblos was not without conflict. The more nomadic Apaches and Navajos liked to mix it up now and then by raiding Pueblo villages.

West James Street, 1882
Early businesses: TJ Grocery, Henry Springer's Mint Saloon, and the Blake & Kelly Harness Shop. Further west, across Rio Grande Boulevard, is the U.S. Post Office. Courtesy UNM Center for Southwest Research, Albuquerque Museum Photo Archives. PA1978.50.38.

And in 1540, the Spanish conqueror Francisco Vásquez de Coronado sent a force led by Captain Hernando de Alvarado to explore the Rio Grande valley on horseback. For the Pueblo people, the predominantly docile days of raising corn and turkeys were over.

For more than a century, Spaniards and Indians tangled with each other. The Spaniards wanted land, water, and control over religious practice, while the Indians wanted to be left alone. Finally, in 1680, the pueblos unified and rebelled in the Pueblo Revolt. The revolt was organized by Popé, a medicine man of San Juan, and other leaders from the Picuris and Santo Domingo pueblos. The Indians killed missionaries and colonists and sent surviving Spaniards fleeing south down the Rio Grande Valley. For a short while, the Pueblo Indians again lived independently, worshipping their own gods and observing seasonal cycles. However, the Spaniards were not to be turned away, and in the 1690s colonists returned in significant numbers to farm and build villages.

Not long after their return, Albuquerque was proclaimed a settlement on a stretch of truth. Spanish colonial rules stated that an official settlement had to have at least thirty families and a site with good water, arable land, and timber. Each settlement's center was to be a plaza, with streets, a church, and government buildings. An elected council was to oversee judicial affairs.

In 1706 Francisco Cuervo y Valdés, governor of colonial New Mexico, told his superior, the Duke of Alburquerque [*sic*] in Alburquerque, Spain, that his settlement met these requirements. But although Cuervo claimed his settlement had thirty-five families, records show that only twelve to fifteen families lived there. In addition, Albuquerque was not a compact village around a plaza, as Cuervo claimed. Instead, it was a collection of farms spread along the Rio Grande. Cuervo assured the duke that a church had been built, when in fact it was only in progress.

To help win graces, Cuervo named his settlement after the duke. Later, when Spain discovered that Cuervo's "village" did not meet its standards, the authorities turned a blind eye. By that time, Albuquerque was firmly established as a trading center.

From Albuquerque's early days to the end of Spanish rule in 1821, its population increased slowly. By 1820, 2,300 people—most of them farmers—lived in the general area. People tended to raise sheep rather than cattle, and weaving was a thriving trade.

From 1821 to 1846, Mexico ruled New Mexico. Since Spain no longer defended the city, it was a prime target for Navajo attacks. But a turn for the better arrived as well. Mexico opened the territory to foreign commerce, welcoming overland wagon trade from the eastern United States. Traders arrived via the Santa Fe Trail from Missouri and the Camino Real, or Royal Road, an 1,800-mile route from Mexico City. Commerce boomed. Wealth had arrived in Albuquerque. Of the city's newly well-off families, among the most ambitious were the Armijos. Brothers Ambrosio, Francisco, Juan, and Manuel served as magistrates during the 1820s and 1830s. They owned homes and ranches in the valley along the Rio Grande.

In 1848 the United States took control of New Mexico, ending Mexico's rule. Soon after, conflict visited Albuquerque, as Union and Confederate soldiers battled one another near the city during the Civil War. Around this time, the United States starved the Navajo people into submission, stopped their raids, and exiled them to Bosque Redondo, east of Navajo country on the Pecos River. Under army escort, the captive Navajo people walked through Albuquerque on their way into exile, in a march called the Long Walk. In 1868 the Navajo people were allowed to return to their homeland west of Albuquerque. Throughout it all, Albuquerque survived as a gritty frontier town.

By 1900 Albuquerque was split in two: There was Old Town, the current tourist center, and New Town, what is now downtown. The 1900 census stated New Town's population to be 6,326 and Old Town's 1,191. Bernalillo County had a population of 12,042, which within five years rose by 5,000. Most of that growth occurred in New Town.

Central and First, 1895

Looking west on Railroad Avenue, which became Central. Photograph by William H. Cobb. Courtesy Ward Hicks Collection, Albuquerque Museum. PA1982.180.365.

Even in its youth, the city spawned suburbs. Barelas, a Hispanic settlement of many years, lay south of New Town. San Jose, a community of Hispanics and blacks, was east of Barelas. Martinez Town, with its winding streets and adobe houses, lay northeast of New Town. Closer to the Rio Grande were Los Griegos, Los Candelarias, and Los Duranes. In his book *Albuquerque: A Narrative History*, Marc Simmons writes about an advertisement in the August 3, 1905, *Albuquerque Morning Journal*. The ad promoted real estate with a semirural feel: "Have a nice garden, raise your own chickens, keep a horse and a

cow. Bring up a family . . . Be independent . . . Enjoy life while you
live. For you will be a long time dead."

Real estate sales were on their way. The distance between the dis-
parate communities became smaller. People left eastern and midwestern cities for life in the Southwest. Land sold; homes were built. The
railroad system flourished. There were streetcars, horse-drawn bug-
gies, and soon enough motorized vehicles. Wholesale merchants such
as the Charles Ilfeld Company thrived, while small business owners
opened stores.

Stark and Brave

Hodgin Hall, the first building at the University of New Mexico, stands alone on the East Mesa, long before any homes were in sight. 1902. Courtesy UNM Center for Southwest Research, Albuquerque Museum. PA1978.50.716.

By 1909 tuberculosis had descended upon the country. For a cure, many people sought the high altitude and dry air of New Mexico, especially Albuquerque. Some who came for cure and stayed were Clinton P. Anderson, U.S. senator and proponent of the U.S. space program; John F. Simms, New Mexico governor; John Gaw Meem, preeminent architect who blended Spanish and Pueblo building styles to create "Santa Fe style"; and William Randolph Lovelace, founder of Lovelace Hospital. All the while, New Mexico was still a territory, not to become a state until 1912.

By this time, the Territorial Fair, or New Mexico Agricultural, Mineral, and Industrial Exposition, had been entertaining people in Albuquerque for more than thirty years. Founded in 1881, the exposition became the State Fair in 1912 and has pulled in large audiences ever since. The first hot-air balloon flight took place at the fair in 1882, when Professor Park A. Van Tassel, a saloonkeeper, flew a 30,000-

cubic-foot balloon high into the air. His flight was a precursor to the activity that in the 1970s took Albuquerque by storm, with avid followers creating today's yearly Balloon Fiesta.

The United States entered World War I in 1917, and the war ended in 1918. Postwar recession plagued New Mexico until the mid-1920s. Growth slowed, but not enough to stop Albuquerque from building one of its first skyscrapers, the First National Bank Building, erected in 1922 at Third and Central. The radio station KGGM aired Albuquerque's first radio program in 1928. The Albuquerque Airport opened in 1928 at what is now Kirtland Air Force Base.

The University of New Mexico had been conceived in 1889, and in 1892 began operations out of one stark Victorian-style building, Hodgin Hall, on the East Mesa. Over the next two decades, a few dormitories and additional halls were built. In 1927 the university campus began to expand, with a sampling of southwestern architectural styles such as Spanish pueblo and territorial.

Downtown Nights

Central Avenue and First Street was the place to be during the 1920s, with automobiles and business signs lit by neon. Courtesy Albuquerque National Bank's Albuquerque Progress Collection, Albuquerque Museum. PA1980.184.82.

(left) **Central and First, 1925**
Streetcar tracks, early model automobiles, and businesses galore: Albuquerque's downtown bustled with activity. Photograph by Cobb Studio. Courtesy Ward Hicks Collection, Albuquerque Museum. PA1982.180.361.

(bottom left) **Resting Station, 1925**
Steam-powered trains await passengers in front of the train depot and the Alvarado Hotel. People from midwestern and eastern cities came often to enjoy Albuquerque's clean air and sunny days. Courtesy Ward Hicks Collection, Albuquerque Museum. PA1982.181.98.

(below) **Working on the Railroad**
Members of the rail yard crew who serviced the great locomotives of the Atchison, Topeka and Santa Fe Railway lines in Barelas. Late 1920s to early 1930s. Courtesy Bueno Foods.

(left) Before the Building Boom

Viewed from East Central Avenue and University Avenue, with the Southeast Heights to the right, the university campus appears sparse. 1932. Photograph by Three Hawks. Courtesy Albuquerque Bernalillo County Public Library System, Albuquerque Museum. PA1978.141.218.

(left below) Opening Night

In 1939 the Lobo Theater opened its doors to a group of eager moviegoers, during the beginning of the city's great expansion. Courtesy Ward Hicks Collection, Albuquerque Museum. PA1982.180.744.

Red Chile Ristras and Four Generations

Members of the Baca family (Teofilo Jojola, Marcus Baca and baby Marie Adele, and Filomena Jojola Baca) pose, reflecting a life in the Middle Rio Grande Valley dedicated to agriculture and chile harvesting. Circa 1930s. Courtesy Bueno Foods.

Lots for Sale
Real estate agent, former mayor, and secretary of the Territorial Fair Association Colonel D. K. B. Sellers and his dog stand at the future site of Albuquerque's first shopping center and the Nob Hill suburb in the Southeast Heights. 1940. Courtesy Albuquerque Public Library Collection, Albuquerque Museum. PA1978.141.282.

By 1930 the city's population had grown to 26,570, with 45,430 people in Bernalillo County. In the late 1930s, Albuquerque began to prosper, and as the United States entered World War II, the city became a major center for military training and weapons research and development. To accommodate the increasing surge of people, the Albuquerque Municipal Airport—boasting then one of the longest runways in the country—opened at its current site in 1939. By 1940 the city's population had grown to 35,449; Bernalillo County's to 69,631.

Kirtland Field, now Kirtland Air Force Base, was constructed adjacent to the municipal airport in 1941. It grew into a major defense installation during the war. On July 15, 1945, the first atomic bomb was tested at White Sands Missile Range, its blast traveling to Albuquerque, where it blew out windows and shook people from their beds. In 1949 Sandia National Laboratories was created near the air base. It brought in hundreds of scientists and engineers to help build the country's weapons stockpile. Since then, the labs have become one of the city's largest employers, working not only in weapons management but also in technological advancements and energy research and development.

Housing subdivisions had begun their crawl toward the Sandia Mountains by 1950. In the late 1940s, Nob Hill Center opened as Albuquerque's first shopping center, followed in 1961 by Winrock Center with its giant enclosed mall. The 1960 census recorded the city population at 201,189 and the county at 262,199.

Homes by the Dozen
Homes were in high demand in the 1950s, during one of the city's biggest population increases. The East Mesa began to fill in with additions such as Dale Bellamah's development. 1950. Courtesy Albuquerque National Bank's Albuquerque Progress Collection, Albuquerque Museum. PA1980.186.75.

(above) **Central and First, Looking West, 1951**
Downtown attracted shoppers and businesspeople. Photograph by Caplin &
Thompson. Courtesy Albuquerque National Bank's Albuquerque Progress Collection,
Albuquerque Museum. PA1980.186.753.

(top right) **Pulling in the Crowds, 1957**
From wrestling to Roller Derby to Chubby Checker or James Brown, the Civic
Auditorium offered it all. Courtesy Albuquerque National Bank's Albuquerque
Progress Collection, Albuquerque Museum. PA1980.187.613.

(bottom right) **Panorama**
Viewed from a rooftop near Third and Gold, Albuquerque High School takes center
stage as the city grows east from its downtown roots. 1950. Courtesy Ward Hicks
Collection, Albuquerque Museum. PA1982.180.433.

Movies under the Stars
The Terrace Drive-In Theater at 9500 East Central, a favorite haunt for nighttime entertainment, is now torn down and only a memory. Courtesy Albuquerque National Bank's Albuquerque Progress Collection, Albuquerque Museum. PA1980.186.796.

City growth had jumped the river, with development plans spreading west. Was there water available to support such growth? Though people of the Sandia Pueblo, just north of the city, called their home Na-fi-at, which in the Tiwa language means Dusty Place, developers and politicians discounted this matter-of-fact observation. Scientists said the city sat on a 10,000-foot-deep trough built of silt, gravel, rocks, and boulders and formed a couple of billion years ago. Some said the trough held enough water to support what could be the Southwest's largest city, one bigger than Las Vegas or Denver. City developers bet on the water. Tract by tract, homes were built upon the dry, dusty mesas on both sides of the river. The water was not as plentiful as hoped, but not knowing that made the future seem bright.

As city growth careened without regulation, the city's aesthetic appeal was weakened. In 1970 the beautiful Alvarado Hotel, a famed

The Mall Arrives, 1962
Winrock Center, the city's first indoor shopping mall, offered a new twist. Photograph by Dick Kent. Courtesy Ward Hicks Collection, Albuquerque Museum.
PA1982.181.373.

Fred Harvey rail station establishment, was torn down and replaced with a parking lot. This incident seemed to wake the public from its trance: Progress needed reining in. Rioting that shook the town in the early 1970s, with civil rights and Vietnam War protests, manifested into eventual change. In 1975 the city enacted its first plan to protect historic landmarks, curb urban sprawl, and control pollution. The Fair Housing Ordinance allowed people of color to buy or rent any house they could afford. The city tried to lure people away from the suburbs and back into downtown, though the public was not persuaded.

By the end of the decade, celebration rang throughout the city for three Albuquerque men, Maxie Anderson, Ben Abruzzo, and Larry Newman, who had crossed the Atlantic in a helium balloon named *Double Eagle II*. It was 1978. The city had grown to a population of more than 300,000, with the county at 420,000.

From that time to today, Albuquerque has strengthened its preservation and conservation movements. Cultural, historical, and environmental associations actively protect the city's valued resources. The Rio Grande bosque is off-limits to building. The Indian Pueblo Cultural Center, owned and operated by nineteen surrounding pueblos, educates the public on Native culture and history. The Albuquerque Museum showcases city history and art. The Museum of Natural History, the Rio Grande Nature Center, and the new National Hispanic Cultural Center are other important institutions. Photography, archaeology, architecture, and music flourish in Albuquerque.

Today, homes butt against the Sandia Mountains and pass the western lava flow, Petroglyph Park, and the western horizon. But the city's character remains intact. Renovation programs have brought new life to poverty-stricken areas. For instance, the Barelas neighborhood, one of Albuquerque's oldest Hispanic settlements, was a trading center on the Camino Real, long before the city was recognized by Spain. It was later home to the Atchison, Topeka and Santa Fe rail yard, where great locomotives were serviced. Blighted by the mid-1900s, the neighborhood has recently cleaned its streets and resurrected old businesses and dining establishments like the Red Ball Café. The mayor holds regular meetings at the Barelas Coffee House. There is life here, in a place that helped give Albuquerque its name as a crossroads town.

In 2006 Albuquerque thrives, with people coming from or going to other parts of the country or other parts of the world, and a person can again walk on Fourth Street, south from downtown into Barelas, and feel a sense of authenticity and living history.

References
Much of the data and statistics in this historical overview come from these sources:

Alberts, Don. *Balloons to Bombers: Aviation in Albuquerque 1882–1945*. Albuquerque: Albuquerque Museum, 1987.

Anella, Anthony. *Never Say Goodbye: The Albuquerque Rephotographic Survey Project*. Albuquerque: Albuquerque Museum, 2001.

Rosner, Hy and Joan. *Albuquerque's Environmental Story: Educating for a Sustainable Community*. Albuquerque: Albuquerque Conservation Association/Albuquerque Planning Department, 1996.

Sanchez, Joseph P. *A History of Early Colonial New Mexico*. Albuquerque: Albuquerque Museum, 1987.

Simmons, Marc. *Albuquerque: A Narrative History*. Albuquerque: University of New Mexico Press, 1982.

Simmons, Marc. *New Mexico: An Interpretive History*. Albuquerque: University of New Mexico Press, 1988.

Surviving Columbus: The Story of the Pueblo People. Video recording. Albuquerque: KNME-TV/Institute of American Indian Art, 1992.

Usner, Don. *New Mexico: Route 66 on Tour*. Santa Fe: Museum of New Mexico Press, 2001.

The Beloved KiMo Theatre
A night at the movies in 1930. Photograph by Brooks Studio. Courtesy Albuquerque Museum. PA1978.151.860.

Treasure

Youth in Albuquerque

Loretta Armenta was born in 1944 in Santa Fe, where she spent her childhood before going to boarding school in Albuquerque. She is president of Qwest New Mexico. She served as a member of Fannie Mae's Housing Impact Advisory Council, on Governor Bill Richardson's Transition Team, and on the New Mexico/Chihuahua Economic Commission. President Bill Clinton appointed her to serve on the North American Development Bank Community Adjustment and Investment Program Advisory Committee. She was president of the Albuquerque Hispano Chamber of Commerce from 1997 to 2004.

I grew up in Santa Fe but went to high school in Albuquerque. I spent my first year at Menaul High School in 1959. [The Presbyterian Church opened the school in 1896 and has run it ever since.]

Loretta Armenta

Girls' Sextette
Loretta Sanchez Armenta (front) and friends in their Menaul High School years, ca. early 1960s. Courtesy Menaul School

What a rude awakening I was in for, after living in a small, protected community like Santa Fe, having to interact with students from Russia, Thailand, Africa, and Albuquerque. One of the things I remember the most was that because we were boarders and living in another kind of protected academic atmosphere, you weren't really allowed to leave campus, but on weekends you and your classmates could go into town on Saturday. You could leave after your chores were done. By nine o'clock you could go and be back by five o'clock. It used to be great because besides Saturday and Sunday, the only other interaction we had outside of school was crossing Menaul and going to the Zanios Foods stand. After school we'd run across the street to get an RC Cola, salted peanuts, and a candy bar. That was the highlight every day!

One Saturday we decided we would be somewhat brave. So not having any transportation and not knowing how to use the bus system or anything like that, we left Menaul and walked up Edith to Lomas. Walking through the Martinez Town neighborhood was very nostalgic for me because it reminded me of Santa Fe. There was a little grocery store, and we walked in there and there was a church [San Ignacio] on a hill. Being Catholic and being in a Presbyterian boarding school sometimes was hard. Well, there were three of us, and we all were ironically Catholic, and we stopped by and went into the church—I still remember it seeming so big and up high on a hill—and we were awed by the church and everything in it. We said our prayers, then walked on and headed to Lomas. We found our way by always asking the question of passersby: "How do we get to downtown?" So we walked to Central, where the old library was, then headed west. Oh my God! Lionel's was there, and we'd heard a lot about Lionel's from the older students. Lionel's Drive-In was *the* spot! It's still there actually. Being all of fifteen years old and in the big city and always being attracted by the unknown, we decided we'd go. There were all these cool kids from Albuquerque High in their cool cars with Bo Diddley playing in the background. So we ordered French fries and soda because that's all we could afford, and watched all of this in amazement. A couple of guys came over and struck up conversation with us. We thought we were really cool. We decided if we were going to finish our journey, we'd better go, though we would have loved to stay at Lionel's, talking to boys for the rest of the day.

We made our way down Central, and we passed the old Alvarado Hotel—it was pretty incredible—and there was another hotel with a big fountain. We saw McClellan's Five and Dime. It was a humongous place! Then we went into Fedway department store. I remember being fascinated by all these stores. It was finally time for us to go, so we went back up Central to Lionel's—we had to stop there again— and by this time it was later in the day, and there was an older crowd. They didn't pay too much attention to us . . . they just thought we were these young teenyboppers. So after that we walked all the way back. Albuquerque was so small then.

Winrock came alive that year, 1961. That was a big deal. I thought it was really special because I hadn't traveled out of New Mexico to stores. There was a restaurant there called Diamond Jim's, with booths with high backs and red and gilt wallpaper—it was like what I had seen in western movies! I was also a candy striper at Presbyterian Hospital. It was very small, but I remember very warmly some of the events they would put together at Christmastime at the Civic Auditorium. Oh, the Civic Auditorium was just great. Later I saw Fats Domino there when I was twenty-one. At that time the beatnik movement was going, and there was a place on Central called the Purple Turk. The Purple Turk—now that was quite an experience, enough where I didn't stay there long!

I returned to Santa Fe when I graduated and came back to live in Albuquerque in 1973 with my husband. Albuquerque is home. It's where our children grew up, went to college, got married, and had children. I feel a cultural richness more here than in Santa Fe, where Hispanics used to be the majority; now they are not. And here we have the richness of the Native Americans and many other people of ethnic backgrounds. It's a city where people for the most part get along very well.

Rubén Cobos graduated from the University of New Mexico with a master's degree in Spanish. He received his doctor of letters from New Mexico Highlands University and taught at UNM for more than thirty years, with additional teaching positions at Stanford University and the University of Nevada at Reno. He is the author of Refranes: Southwestern Spanish Proverbs and A Dictionary of New Mexico and Southern Colorado Spanish (MNM Press).

Rubén Cobos

Words of Wisdom in Spanish
In his dictionary of Spanish from another era, Rubén Cobos unveils the beauty and charm of a language still spoken in northern New Mexico. Courtesy Rubén Cobos.

I've been here in the twenties, the thirties, the forties, the fifties, the sixties, the seventies, the eighties, the nineties . . . until now. I was born November 11, 1911—that's 11/11/11! When I was five years old, living in Mexico, I remember we heard about Pancho Villa going into Columbus [New Mexico]. All of us were excited. His *muchachos* went crazy, we heard. But all his soldiers did was shoot at tin cans and stray cats. They were just having fun. The first time we [his mother, two sisters, and grandmother] came here was in 1925. We were living in San Antonio, Texas, then. We thought Albuquerque was quite a city. We came to see a Mr. Pablo Camarillo . . . he lived in Barelas at Third Street and Lead. There was a streetcar driven by a great big lady. And I befriended her. I went to her and told her I was from San Antonio. She drove us up East Central as far as the university. I remember Hodgin Hall, the library, and a building for engineers. We went back to San Antonio and came back four years later, in 1929. My mother, a sister, and I came to see my older sister, who was very sick at the Presbyterian Sanatorium, which was the beginning of Presbyterian Hospital. She had tuberculosis and had been a missionary for five years until she got sick. She died here in Albuquerque. So we just stayed, and I've been here ever since.

I finished elementary school at Menaul School and stayed until I graduated from high school. I was valedictorian at Menaul. Then, in 1932, I went to the University of New Mexico. My mother was a seamstress. She could make anything; she worked in the Sunshine Laundry. At that time I had nothing in my mind other than I was going to go to the university. I started walking from First Street. I didn't ride the bus, which was drawn by a huge mule. Our house was two blocks west of Presbyterian Hospital . . . we moved on to Martinez Town later. It was very early in the morning when I started walking to see what a university was. I stood in front of a long, tall building [Hodgin Hall]. So I went back down again and had lunch with my mother. She had a job for me in the Sunshine Laundry, and I said no, I'm going to the university. She said we didn't have any money. I said I would get a job at the university. I was sure I was going to get a job.

Well, back at Menaul School, Mr. Donaldson was superintendent. He had a system, a beautiful setup with students, with about 125 young boys and men. He divided students into squads of about twelve students, and my squad for two weeks would be cooks in the dining room. We learned everything about being cooks, setting tables; we learned what you'd expect a person in a restaurant to do. Then we would work out in the field milking cows, taking care of the horses . . . we had corn and all kinds of vegetables, and for another two weeks, we were farmers. We were carpenters, too. We learned to make boxes, chairs, and benches. This was repeated from 1929 to 1932, so I knew it very well! Later, the school did this with the girls when my wife was there, but I was no longer there. This was how I was formed. So when I went to the university, I went directly to the president. I didn't know there were other steps I should have taken, and I talked to Dr. James

Fulton Zimmerman. I said, "I'm here to tell you I'm coming to the university in September." He was glad and showed me to the door.

"There's something I forgot to tell you: What will I use for money?" I asked him. I told him I was good at lawns, taking care of trees, beautiful flowers. I told him what I did for years at Menaul School. I'm a carpenter, cook, dining-room waiter.

"Okay," he said. "You'll get a job." He gave me a slip of paper with the name of the head of maintenance written on it.

Oh, the head of maintenance was mad when he saw that piece of paper. He said I had no business going to the president. But he put me to work as a carpenter. I decided to get into Spanish—I grew up speaking Spanish in Mexico—as a major, and English as a minor. Another minor was the history of New Mexico. I graduated in 1936 and started teaching . . . I had a specialty to teach high school. I had a chance to teach in Albuquerque, but I didn't want to. I told my mother I wanted to go out to the villages, so I took a job in Wagon Mound. I came down to Albuquerque for a teachers' state convention in 1937 and gave a speech on teaching and methodology in Spanish, the Spanish of literature. Two gentlemen [the director of Highlands University and a Spanish professor from Chile] approached me after it and asked where I was teaching and if I'd like to teach at Highlands University. I taught there from 1937 to 1940. In 1941 I was drafted. Then, when the war was over, I came back to Albuquerque and was walking the grounds around Hodgin Hall reminiscing—I'm ninety-four years old and I forget things. Let's see, Dr. Kirtchwell, the head of the language department, came out and said he wanted me at UNM. That's when it started. I taught there from 1945 until I retired in 1976.

During that time, I wrote books on languages. The interest came from going into all the small villages of northern New Mexico. I'd hear sixteenth-century Spanish. My students spoke it. I talked to them [about their Spanish], and they invited me to their homes, and I spent the weekends. I would hear them speaking. I was very interested. My wife, Vira, was born in Taos, and her family spoke sixteenth-century

Spanish. Even before I went to the university, I was very interested in listening to my classmates, and I would cut little pieces of paper and put those words on them with their meanings. I loved listening to the old Spanish.

Pete V. Domenici was born May 7, 1932, in Albuquerque. After graduating from the University of New Mexico, he tried his hand as a minor-league baseball pitcher for the Albuquerque Dukes. He went on to law school at the University of Denver and returned to Albuquerque, where he practiced law for fourteen years. He served on the City Commission before being elected to the U.S. Senate. He is the first New Mexican to serve six full six-year terms as a senator. He was named a Notable New Mexican by the Albuquerque Museum Foundation in 2005.

My mom and dad had a house in Los Candelarias on Candelaria Boulevard going west. It was an old brick and stucco. I was born in this house. I was a big baby—ten pounds—and when my mother held me up, she said I looked like a bocci ball, so I got the name Bocci.

My father recalled that upon his arrival [from Italy in 1906 or 1907], though Old Town was the center of town, the railroad station was the center of all activity. There was one road that had a surface, First Street, and he said the road was covered with wood! [Planks had been laid to benefit pedestrians during rains.] My dad's business was the Montezuma Grocery Company at First and Lomas. The wholesale grocery business took a lot of work, all done by the family. We sold to small stores in Gallup, Socorro, Tijeras, but not to Santa Fe. I worked there every summer after I was thirteen, and so did my cousins. When I graduated from college in 1954, my parents sold the business. My dad felt I wouldn't be able to take it over. It was the advent of chain stores, and he saw big change. So rather than borrow money [to enlarge the store to be competitive], they sold. I feel bad about that, but he came to the right conclusion.

Pete V. Domenici

When I was working [in tenth grade], I wasn't as big as the workingmen, and I'd go out in a truck to another wholesaler, Charles Ilfeld. My dad wouldn't know what I did there. There was a man, and he'd

see me and know who I was. He knew my dad and knew the implications. He'd say, "You go over there and go to sleep. I'll wake you up; you're too little. We'll tell your dad that you worked hard." That was pretty nice.

I also remember when I was in fifth grade we moved to the old country club area. St. Mary's was a grade school, and it had an open field, the only place we had to practice football, and there was a little gym. As I recollect . . . I had a big, big joy. The school had an outside fire escape, and in the summer we would go there and slide down. We would take my mother's wax paper, walk up in bare feet, and slide down on that.

The Italian families would meet a lot. Eventually they formed a club, the Cristoforo Colombo Lodge—it was mainly for older men. It would be open all day Sunday, and the men would go to play poker and pitch—that's a card game. I'd sit on the floor and watch. Our young lives were built around the church, home [and social activities among Italian American families]. My father worked six days a week, and mother was active and outgoing. She would do anything for her kids. She had the biggest heart.

This was back in 1942 or 1943, and Italian Americans were similar to but not as suspect as Japanese Americans. They were looked upon with suspicion. Here, after all the things my mother did [she worked for school charities and other civic organizations], she was not a U.S. citizen. Marriage did not make her a citizen. One day, the immigration service arrived at our backyard with all their pomp and black cars. They wanted to know if she was Mrs. Domenici, and they said, "You're under arrest for being an illegal alien." Well, before they could accomplish the mission, the next-door neighbors called the lawyer, Senior John Simms. The old man Simms was an Arkansas guy with a big southern accent. He got to the house before they took her; he gave them plenty of static. He made them take him with her. They didn't want to, but he insisted. But they also took my dad's shotgun and disassembled our brand-new Zenith—it had a shortwave in it. They let her come home that same night. She had to study [to become a U.S. citizen and was granted citizenship]. I was very impressionable then, and I can see it all now.

Debra Hughes was born in Alamogordo, New Mexico, on October 3, 1955, and grew up in Albuquerque from age one. Her short fiction has been anthologized in Tierra: Contemporary Short Fiction of New Mexico *and* Walking the Twilight: Women Writers of the Southwest *and has also appeared in* New Letters, New Mexico Humanities Review, *and* Blue Mesa Review. *A frequent contributor to* New Mexico Magazine, *Hughes won the 2002 Silver Award for Reader Service given by the International Regional Magazine Association. Her essays about New Mexico's generations-old general stores were part of a 2003 exhibition at the Museum of New Mexico's Palace of the Governors. Hughes has taught at Ohio State University, where she received a master of arts in English literature. A former literature associate with Western States Arts Federation, she has judged literary competitions for the states of Colorado, Utah, and Wyoming and has led writing workshops.*

The tom turkey snapped its wing feathers and charged after my fingers wiggling through fence wire. I stepped back, thankful to be on the other side. The thing was a brute, and I a kid of eleven, wishing for might. My parents had recently bought Bill and Margaret Kitsch's back pasture, where we built our home, and that day I was prying. The Kitsches raised turkeys and collected wagon wheels and wagons, the kind of wagons that people had traveled in from Mexico or across the Great Plains, and the

Searching for Treasure
Debra Hughes, May 1970, with Ovid and Dun Dee.

Debra Hughes

relics were grouped under the shade of elm trees near the Kitsches' two-story adobe. Mr. Kitsch came at me carrying a shovel. It was summer, irrigating season. He pushed dirt with that shovel to channel water from ditches into his pasture, and he also dug around a lot. Tall, he had a shock of red hair under a sweat-rimmed cowboy hat, and with a red goatee, he easily passed in my mind as Wild Bill Hickok. "There are fossils as big as turkeys down there," he said and pointed to the ground. Story was that dragonflies with wingspans of thirty inches and giant cockroaches lived in this valley long before the Rio Grande flowed just west of us. He was going to dig up one of those fossilized insects, and the find would make him rich. There was treasure buried beneath our feet.

I imagined instant wealth, and its lure guided me to banks of the "dirty ditch," used for irrigating alfalfa fields and vegetables, and to the "clear ditch." More stream than ditch, its water came from the Rio Grande north of Albuquerque and the cottonwood groves in between. These ditches ran parallel to the Rio Grande and right behind our house in Albuquerque's North Valley. As it turned out, we built our home on the old Kitsch dumping ground, a potpourri on its own. We uncovered worn cowboy boots, cow bones and the bones of a dog, medicine bottles, and tin cans, tools, barbed wire, nuts, bolts, and most often nails—all rusted. From the back pasture grew two fat cottonwoods, wild asparagus, red willow. There was shade and a pitch and roll to it, where wild game birds took cover and roadrunners whacked snakes to death for dinner. It was not in my backyard where I knew I would strike it rich. It was on the ditch.

Smell gives age away, and I smelled it in the dirt, layers upon layers of river silt and who knows what rotting. Even our well water back at the house tasted as if it had been mixing with something that had died long ago. I dug where an exposed tree root seemed more like bone than plant. I wasn't after prehistoric insects, but a woolly mammoth tusk would do.

When my feet wouldn't take me far enough, I rode my horse, a brood mare as round as a pumpkin and named Ovid. The Roman poet, author of *Metamorphoses*, might have found the naming a natural change when some local horse breeders bestowed his name upon a mare. Nevertheless, I rode my Goddess of Love along those ditch banks and through miles and miles of bosque. Secretly, mine was an ancient kingdom. I drew from elementary school history class taught by Mr. Pack, a tall pale man whose cheeks reddened and eyes watered when recounting our state's history. Was he going to cry at the part when Coronado sent his men from Spain in search of cities of gold but met instead Pueblo Indians farming maize? Our history book didn't tell us what Mr. Pack probably suspected: The Indians were killed, their corn stolen. I sensed tragedy, joy, and many things yet to be revealed. There were history gaps; to fill in, I populated my ditch rides with Ice Age horses, Desert Hunters, Basket Makers, parrots from ancient Mexico, all of them active in my mind as I roamed atop my horse. There were copper bells and feather plumes in armor and of course dinosaurs, all in one mix. Such panoply. I could not resist edging it with a bit of danger. Imaginary eyes watched from brush and tree. Though certain I had the cunning to tackle most anything, when the stares became too intense, I'd egg my horse into an all-out gallop, flying down the ditch path, bareback, with horse sweat stinging my thighs. We were fast.

On a day hot enough to make dirt crack into puzzle pieces, Jimmy, Mr. Kitsch's grandson, came for a visit. The thin boy with hair cut short by electric clippers walked through the Kitsch pasture into ours. He was headed for the ditch. Maybe he was nine. I was not the babysitting sort, mothering dolls not strong in my heart. But I asked anyway. "Do you know how to swim?"

When he said no, I said I'd show him the ditch, but he couldn't get in the water. I'd overheard my parents say the boy lived with his mother in the Sandia Mountains, the range that framed our eastern horizon, which explained his unfamiliarity with the ditch and river world. I led him down my path through thick red willow clumps. I told him to place his feet when walking where others had been, so no one could track us. Though I kept it to myself, I was certain I was the kind of Indian I had read about in books who could outrun and outsmart any predator, man or beast. Without realizing it, I had invited him into my imaginary world, for at that time in my life the physical and the fanciful were tied tightly together. "No one's after us," he said and clumped his feet along, setting them anywhere, leaving tracks in plain sight. That he would not see or feel what I did bothered me. This was my place, and he the unappreciative outsider. I wanted him to go home.

He darted for the ditch bank. The water, its usual chocolate brown, rolled by, moving abandoned tires, small tree limbs, whatever people upstream tossed in hoping not to see again. Clods of horse dung were coming our way. He could take the one in front, I said, and I bet on the one spinning in an eddy. The finish line was where we stood, and his won the race. I had hoped that would satisfy him so I could lead him back to his grandfather's home. But Jimmy was fast and on his stomach with arms stretched to touch water. The bank's incline was steep. Ploop! Frogs and toads make that sound too when they land in water. Jimmy went under, popped up, and went under again. On his next rise I grabbed his hand and pulled him out. I didn't even walk him all the way back home. I took him to the fence dividing our pastures. "Run" I told him. Shivering, with wet clothes sticking to his tiny frame, he took off.

I never thought to tell, not that telling would get him or me into trouble, but Jimmy could have drowned. On the ditch a sure footing was never sure. And with Jimmy's fall, so too slipped my fantasy. Mr. Kitsch wasn't digging for treasure; he just wanted me to stop pestering his turkeys. That I thought I could discover something bigger and thus better than a fossilized bug was a bit embarrassing. That I wanted to get rich off it wasn't something I wanted to discuss with my parents. On my own, I let illusions disperse.

Back in the mid- to late 1960s, Albuquerque was in full bloom. On what had once been barren mesa rising east to the mountains, sun reflected from windows and roofs. In our den, Mr. and Mrs. Kitsch joined my parents for cocktails, he with mud-splattered cowboy boots and she in a gingham blouse and slacks. She moved like the birds they raised, head held high and alert to action around her. Standing, she came midway to her husband's chest. They took Scotch on ice with water, as did my parents. And they talked about water. The city had jumped the river with development plans spreading west. Was there water available to support such growth? The city's leaders believed there was. My folks and the Kitsches did not. Now, forty years later, geologists are finding water more of a valuable scarce resource than one of plenty.

Today, the city attracts newcomers and businesses, and amid the construction, the past is undeniable. The name Albuquerque dates from Roman times, when the original site in Spain was named Alba-quercus, a derivation of the Latin *albus quercus,* or "white oak." The Spanish municipality's coat of arms, a white oak on a crimson field, uncannily resembles the Rio Grande's cottonwoods. The past hangs along the river as a presence, like a reclusive neighbor, unseen but felt. It whirls on daily winds around the ancient river cottonwoods with leaves as big as a woman's hands. Like it or not, everyone who lives here knows he or she is not the first. Exactly who was first remains a mystery. Native Indian tribes tell ancient stories. They have hunted, fished, had babies, grown corn, illustrated life's adventure on scattered rock, prayed, danced, and died here. Vastly different cultures— Pueblo, Apache, Navajo, and Spanish—have rubbed against each other. Some have taken turns massacring each other, and always the river has flowed, shallow or gorged. Its floods have pushed heavy silt over crops and sites where people were buried. It's not uncommon for road construction to stop when a burial site is uncovered and the remains are tended to. Backyards frequently become roped-off archaeological digs after gardeners have unearthed human bones and relics. Historians say people have been here for at least 20,000 years— evidence having been preserved in the earth's sedimentary layers. And, yes, with a trained eye a person can find fossilized traces of those giant dragonflies of much earlier geologic periods. After another great expanse of time, will these homes and freeways and downtown buildings become bedrock for other structures, mulch for future riverbank growth?

After Jimmy's visit, my summers passed in their slow, meandering way. Friends joined in ditch rides. If any eyes stared from behind bushes, they belonged to boys, not to imaginary creatures watching us girls in our bikinis swim our horses across the deeper clear ditch. One July night when we were seventeen, Sally, Susan, Trip, Mike, Doug, Coby, and I rode at midnight down Chavez Road, across Rio Grande Boulevard to the ditch. No one was out for a drive at that hour; the full moon illuminated our way. We rode in silence. When we got to the cottonwood grove nearest my home, we entered its darkness. Trees with giant girths and arching limbs pitched their eerie shadows. We nudged our horses faster and slipped into a clearing where little grew. The clear sky and moon seemed close enough to touch. Sharing an unspoken cue, we circled our horses and galloped at full speed around and around. Only then did we holler and hoot at lung capacity. It was a ritual we knew instinctively. Like the souls before us, we were in a kingdom in a celebration of night. When the horses broke sweat we stopped. Crickets, frogs, and distant coyotes sounded. We turned back and rode in single file silently until we reached the barn. It was a good ride, we all agreed.

Al Hurricane was born in Dixon, New Mexico, in 1936. He came to Albuquerque in 1947. The Norman Petty Studio in Clovis, New Mexico, has recorded his music, as has Challenge Records and his own studio, Hurricane Records. While he plays in Europe and across the United States, much of his time is spent entertaining audiences throughout New Mexico.

I was eleven [in 1948] when I started playing at La Placita in Old Town. I used to sit on the wishing well and play for tips. After a while, the owner asked me to rove through the restaurant as a troubadour. My father taught me guitar, and he and I played in our own program on the Spanish station, KVER, until I was thirteen. Then I was known as Little Albert Sanchez, but Mom

Al Hurricane

High Notes
Al Hurricane has played with legends like Fats Domino, James Brown, and Chuck Berry, and he still draws crowds to his own brand of Latin and pop music. Courtesy Al Hurricane.

used to call me Hurricane because I used to knock things over. The name stuck, so eventually I took it as my professional name.

When I was fifteen, we got a group together. We were called the Sentimentalists. We had no leader, and we played for only one dance with three couples. The guys didn't seem too serious, and we busted the band up right after the dance. Then a few of us [Al and his younger brothers Amador and Gabriel, professionally known as Tiny Morrie and Baby Gaby] got a chance to play at a hamburger drive-in at Coors and Central. We were called Al Hurricane and His Night Rockers. We played at the Heights Community Center, Oasis Dance Hall, and YMCA at Central and First. This guy by the name of Richard Chavez came up to me after one of the dances and asked if he could help. So he rented the Old Town Society Hall and had a concert. We had eight hundred people. He said he wouldn't be our manager, but he just wanted to expose us to the crowds. Then along came Mike London—do you remember Mike London? He was a wrestling promoter, and he got us playing twice a week at places. When the Civic Auditorium opened up in 1957, we opened it with 2,500 people. Mr. Swan, the manager of the Civic Auditorium, said, "You know what? Mike is a wrestling promoter. He's making money off that and you. I'd like to set up some teen dances here—you can sign, right?" I was not old enough, so my mother came up and signed for me. She signed for twenty-four dates.

Well, that led to her becoming a big-time music promoter! Her name is Bernie L. Sanchez. She's promoted Elvis Presley, James Brown, the Dave Clark Five, Fats Domino, the Animals, Antonio Aguilar, Chubby Checker, Marty Robbins, and Jimmy Clanton—he was supposed to be the best-looking man in America, and the girls would faint in his audience. Once, Chuck Berry was here playing at the Civic. He was in a fight with his manager, and my mother stepped up to calm him down, and he handed me his guitar, which was worth thousands of dollars and which no one played. Well, I started playing it, and he turned around and looked at me! When he went on stage, he asked me to come on, too, and he let me play his Wurlitzer. He started playing "Teenage Wedding," and I played along with him. He stopped and I kept playing. He turned around and let me play a solo. It was something else.

Though I played rock and roll—I toured with Fats Domino, who influenced me a lot—I still hold on to my Latin roots from the La Placita days. We built our company, Hurricane Records, on a mix of Latin and Top 40. We have fifty-one LPs or CDs. We [he and son Al Hurricane Jr.] try to keep up with the Top 40, whether it's rock and roll or hip-hop. We play "Ladies Night," "The Twist," "Johnny Be Good," and "Bad Mama Jama."

But, you know, in high school I never was a big hit. I went to Albuquerque High—those are some of my better memories. You remember those days. What I did was music, and I always wished I were popular like the quarterback! Now when I go to Denny's or Furr's, people come up to me and ask for my autograph. It means a lot to me.

Helen R. Lucero was born in northern New Mexico and has called Albuquerque home for over forty years. She is director of visual arts at the National Hispanic Cultural Center of New Mexico. She was associate curator at the Smithsonian's National Museum of American Art, curator of Hispanic arts for the University of New Mexico Art Museum, and curator of southwestern Hispanic folk art with the Museum of International Folk Art in Santa Fe. There, she oversaw the exhibition Familia y Fe, *Lucero's legacy to her New Mexican Hispanic ancestry. She coauthored* Chimayo Weaving: The Transformation of a Tradition *(University of New Mexico Press, 1999) and has received a Rockefeller Foundation Humanities Fellowship.*

I came to Albuquerque in the summer of 1959, when I was fifteen and my sister Sadie was seventeen; she was my guardian. I came from Vadito, a tiny village in northern New Mexico. Our parents were separated, and we needed a way to support ourselves. The fact that I came to the city from a village of about two hundred people was like magic, and the fact that we were on our own was wonderful! We worked as waitresses in restaurants that summer. I worked for Jotter's Ace Café on East Central and Louisiana, near Kirtland Air Force Base. Sadie worked at Walgreens downtown.

Helen R. Lucero

Coming from a community that was very definitely Hispanic to Albuquerque, where there were all these air force guys who knew nothing about Hispanics—there was no discrimination and that was very important—well, it was a wonderful, magical summer spent discovering the city and dating for the first time. My sister and I double-dated quite often. We went to drive-in movies at the Cactus on Yale, the Terrace on Central, and the Duke City. We saw movies such as *Summer Place, The Mating Game, The Miracle,* and *Helen of Troy.* The top single song hit that summer was "Running Bear." We rode around in 1950s cars, going up and down Central, stopping at Bob's Drive-In

An Artist in the Making
Sixteen-year-old Helen R. Lucero poses in one of Albuquerque's photo booths. 1959. Courtesy Helen R. Lucero.

and the Purple Turk. We paid fifteen dollars a month for a tiny basement apartment with overhead water pipes and a dirt floor. But it was one of those summers that I think my sister and I will remember forever. I think that when you are introduced to a city in that kind of magical way, you bond with it and always feel something special about it.

I lived in the Southeast Heights, near the university. One of the curious things is that in Albuquerque I have always lived in the Southeast Heights. I think it's because of some of my early connections . . . it's interesting because this neighborhood and Albuquerque are home, even though I wasn't born here. Whenever I leave New Mexico and when I come back, I'm home. I found my identity here.

In 1960, when I was sixteen, I went to work at the Casa Luna Pizzeria at night and started taking classes at the University of New Mexico during the day. I was the first in my family to go to college and the only one to get a Ph.D. In 1986 I was one of very few Hispanic females to get a Ph.D from UNM. New Mexico Hispanic weaving was the topic of my dissertation. Many of my relatives were weavers. I loved that school, UNM. It was the right place for me.

There's very little I would change in my life. I've done the things I've set out to do: I wanted to have a child, and I did. I wanted to work for the Smithsonian, and I did. I wanted to write a book, and I did. Now I want to paint. That's where I started out, in art. Now, the Hispanic Cultural Center is the place where I can bring together all that I have learned. There's a lot of art taking place here in Albuquerque, and Hispanics are very much a part of that. Here at the center, artists come in to give workshops, lectures, and other educational programs. As the director of the art museum, I can give back now, back to the community. And the fact that Spanish is spoken here at the center, at the church I attend, and among my friends is very important to me. I've lived in places where that was not always so. Albuquerque—it has certainly been a good place to live.

Ada Pecos Melton was born in Albuquerque but raised in the Pueblo of Jemez from birth to adulthood. She is president and owner of American Indian Development Associates, an Indian-owned technical assistance, training, and research firm in Albuquerque that addresses public policy and program development concerning Indian crime and victimization issues. Melton is the recipient of the 2000 New Mexico Distinguished Public Service Award and the 1999 Distinguished Alumni Award from the University of New Mexico Public Administration Department. She was also awarded Outstanding Achievement Recognition for Advancing the Needs of Indian Children from the U.S. Office of Juvenile Justice and Delinquency Prevention in 1998. She is a board member and former president of the American Indian Graduate Center, which funds fellowships and scholarships for Native American graduate students across the country.

My husband is from Laguna Pueblo, and I am from Jemez Pueblo. We came to Albuquerque in 1989, partly for housing and schools for our four kids. It became a good median place. Both

Ada Pecos Melton

my parents are up at Jemez, and all my brothers and sisters live there. I'm the only one who lives in Albuquerque. I go up every weekend and participate in all our feast days. My children are from both pueblos, and they dance and do all that's expected of them at each place. When I go home, there is a switch, where suddenly I'm going by the ways of the pueblo. I think in Jemez but translate in English. If I get stressed from work in the city, I go back to my comfort zone: Jemez.

I came to Albuquerque in my childhood, too. My dad worked at the Utility Block Company, and my family would come in to shop for feast days and to buy clothes for school. Along with shopping, we would get to go to the movies. The KiMo Theatre was the first movie theater I had ever been to. Half the time during the movie, I'd be looking at all those gargoyles on the wall, and I'd even go home and still think about them! I saw *Johnny Be Good, Tora! Tora! Tora!* and all

Clint Eastwood's movies, such as *Fistful of Dollars*. My first major hairdo was in junior high, and I went to the beauty salon next to the KiMo. We didn't know where else to go and had seen the store, so we gave it a try. My hair turned out pretty well!

Before the movies, my dad would drop my mother, brothers, and me off downtown, and we would walk from the KiMo to the Sunshine. We saw *Romeo and Juliet* at the Sunshine, and we got all dressed up like Sunday dress-up to go to it. It was a huge adventure going into Woolworth's to get a soda at the soda fountain, then on to Sears and Bellas Hess. Then, after the movie, we'd stop at McDonald's before driving back home. To this day, my favorite things are the regular hamburger, fries, and an orange soda—it takes me back to when I was eight years old!

I'm appreciative of all things in my life. You get here from other people helping you. My parents told me, "You're going to college. We'll make it work. Freedom is education." So I went. I was working with the Laguna tribal court system while getting my undergraduate degree in criminal justice and a master's in public administration at UNM. A lot of my work at Laguna Pueblo was developing policies and procedures and making sure the staff and judges were trained. I was court administrator and chief probation officer. Then I was asked to set up the court probate system at Taos Pueblo. Before I knew it, I went to other states to do the same. Very quickly I started hiring other consultants, for I couldn't do it alone. From 1989 to 1994, I did my work out of the house. I got a grant to do a study on child abuse and neglect on reservations. The U.S. Department of Health and Human Services awarded me and another nonprofit group, the National Indian Justice Center, almost a half a million dollars because it was a nationwide study. That's when the need to move my office from the house became apparent, so in the mid-1990s, I moved my business [American Indian Development Associates] into the Indian Pueblo Cultural Center. My family said, "We want our living room back!"

I work with the New Mexico Youth and Family Department, helping establish policy for the needs of Indian children. If a youth commits an offense or is hurt, we have established a way for them to get culturally relevant treatment. We build a robust model for each particular tribe on how to establish its own policies reflective of customs, laws, and traditions. We never take control over what each tribe should do. We know we are facilitators, and that keeps the tribes empowered.

It's been a great journey. It's been incredible to get this support from tribal leadership. I've gotten their respect through earning it, the old-fashioned way. We live in Albuquerque, and we're away [from Laguna and Jemez pueblos], but not that far away.

Piggly Wiggly and a Twinkie
Every Saturday, Ada Pecos Melton's family came to Albuquerque from Jemez Pueblo to shop and go to movies. At the end of the day, they would stop at a Piggly Wiggly grocery store and buy a Twinkie for the ride home. "We called it the 'celebration of the Twinkie,'" says Melton. Photograph by Milner Studio. courtesy Albuquerque Museum. PA 1992.5.392

Roberta Cooper Ramo is a graduate of the University of Colorado, with a law degree from the University of Chicago. She practices law with the Modrall Sperling law firm. She became president of the American Bar Association in 1995, the first woman president in the association's history. Ramo also served six years on the University of New Mexico's Board of Regents, including two years as president.

Roberta Cooper Ramo

Blue Jeans and a Life in Law
Roberta Cooper Ramo fondly remembers the smell of new jeans that filled her family's store when she was a child. But the field of law lured her away from selling western merchandise. Courtesy Roberta Cooper Ramo.

Albuquerque was filled with a visual beauty that was profound to me as a child. The skies were huge, the light powerful, and the scent of the air like perfume. When I was ten, I went to the Albuquerque Public Library by myself on the bus. Our city was small enough then and the kind of place where I wouldn't have risked doing anything wrong, because someone would have told my parents! Going to the library was a daylong voyage. The library [at Central and Edith] was an elegant John Gaw Meem structure. It seemed huge, vast, infinite. The librarians allowed me into the adult section. I remember people from pueblos being there, all sorts of teachers, nuns in habits, university students, women with gray hair done up, in gloves and heels. The library required our best behavior. They were very strict about how books were to be treated. You could only take out as many books as you could carry; no dog-earing the pages, and watch the covers, that is, if they were still in service! The librarians challenged the life of the mind and helped inform anyone who ventured inside about New Mexico aesthetics. There was a wonderful sense of the Spanish heritage of New Mexico—art, music, literature—that came across in a very European way. They brought in exhibits from around the world, too. I remember an exhibit of the machines of Leonardo da Vinci. The exhibit sparked my lifelong interest in all things Italian. The library informed my image of being an adult, a New Mexican.

My dad, David Cooper, owned a western wear store. We met all kinds of people there. He traded with Native Americans from many tribes. There were jockeys coming to race at the State Fair, ranchers and cowboys and soldiers from everywhere. It was like being in the world's most interesting railroad terminal. My dad and mom started the business as a small store, and I dusted boots at about six. I felt both important and confident. There's still nothing like the smell of fresh blue jeans and cowboy boots!

No one grows up here without loving the outdoors. It can rain in your front yard, while the sun shines in your backyard. We often had picnics in the mountains. Several families would go up to Doc Long's, and we'd put watermelons in the stream and fish and grill our dinner. This is that rare place where people pull off the highway to enjoy a beautiful sunset.

Growing up Jewish here was also wonderful; I went to my friends' Catholic celebrations, and they came to ours. For someone who is Catholic or Baptist to understand what it is to be Jewish was not an unusual thing for me—it was part of everyday life. For me, hearing the beautiful music at an Episcopal church made me understand the phrase "music to my ears." There is a . . . "connectiveness" here. I think that feeling of wanting to know about others different than you has gotten lost in other places, and I worry it is threatened here. In order to preserve our state's culture, we need to show dignity and respect to everyone.

Albert Simms grew up in Albuquerque with an older brother, John Jr., and a younger sister, Francis Ann. His father was John F. Simms Sr., and his mother was Anne Schluter Simms. He attended public school through eighth grade in Albuquerque, then continued at Fountain Valley School in Colorado. He received his undergraduate degree at the University of New Mexico, graduated from medical school at Columbia University, and completed residencies at Bellevue Hospital and Roosevelt Hospital in New York City. He served as a medical officer during World War II. His surgical practice lasted from 1951 to 1977. During those years, he was a member of the American Medical Association and the New Mexico Medical Society and a fellow of the American College of Surgeons. He has served as a board member of the Fountain Valley School, the Albuquerque Academy for Boys (now Albuquerque Academy), the Museum of New Mexico, and St. John's College in Santa Fe and Annapolis, Maryland. He was also a regent at the University of New Mexico and chairman of the Bernalillo County Indian Hospital Board of Trustees. He and his wife, Barbara Young Simms, have raised five children.

Albert Simms

I was born in 1920 at our home at Twelfth Street and Fruit and delivered by Dr. Lucien Rice. I had my tonsils taken out by Dr. Harry Brehmer at Presbyterian Hospital in 1925. The last room in the hospital was taken during the night, and they put a cot for me in one of the three operating rooms. Little did I know that twenty-five years later, I would have the privilege of operating on Dr. Brehmer. I started school at Fourth Ward School and got along fine. However, in the first grade I played hooky one day with a friend. My friend said his father would take us to lunch, but on the way downtown, we went down an alley to look at pigeons raised by Mr. Gray, the postman. Suddenly, we looked up and saw a man on a horse, and we knew right away it was "Hooky Tom," or Tom Morrow, the school truant officer. He pointed to me and

asked, "What's your name?" I said, "I don't know, but it's not Albert Simms," whereupon he put me and my friend on his horse and took us back to school.

Time passed, and I went through the eighth grade at Washington Junior High. Aunt Ruth Simms asked if I wanted to go to Fountain Valley School in Colorado Springs, a prep school where her son had been enrolled. So off I went for four years, and it was a wonderful experience. I started University of New Mexico in 1937. I then went on in 1940 to medical school at Columbia University. Barbara and I were married in 1943, after graduation, and I began an internship in New York. In 1944 I was in the service as first lieutenant in the Medical Corps and served until 1946. The next year, I began a four-year surgical training program while still in New York City.

In the summer of 1951, Barbara and I wanted to open a practice in Greenwich, Connecticut, but my father, John F. Simms Sr., was diagnosed with angina pectoris. So we returned to Albuquerque, where I opened my surgical practice. My dad was retired from the state supreme court. He was a southerner who had great sympathy for sick people because he and Uncle Albert both had come to Silver City in 1912 with tuberculosis. They were treated in the "Cottage San" by Dr. Bullock, known to be a fine "bug doctor." My father got better in a few months and decided he could not afford room, board, and medical care amounting to seventeen dollars a month. So he went to Albuquerque. The best he could do was a bed on an open porch for a dollar a night across the street from St. Joe's. He didn't have enough money to get back to Silver City, so he opened a small law office and went on from there. Over the years he developed a fine practice. Anyway, this [his father's angina] was before bypass surgery or stent surgery, and the average longevity was four to six years, and he died in 1954. Barbara and I were very happy we had come home and had those years with the family. Shortly thereafter I joined in partnership with Dr. Lawrence Wilkinson and Dr. Vaun Floyd, my former medical school roommate.

Before World War II, many older doctors in Albuquerque were beginning to approach retirement. That's when Albuquerque had a population of 40,000, and there were about a half a dozen middle-aged doctors who would succeed them. Many of these went into the service, and when they returned in '45 and '46, Albuquerque had grown. Many physicians from Albuquerque and from the armed services were looking for a growing community in which to restart their practices. This was a whole new generation. They entered all sorts of specialty practices. We had quite a fellowship. Looking back, I was fortunate to first come on staff at Presbyterian and St. Joseph. I was thrilled to make house calls and was always glad to make the ER call for all the older doctors. I recall my charge for house calls was five dollars to ten dollars. I met some of the most wonderful people, and I'll never forget their plights and the pleasure I had in taking care of them. I still urge young doctors to make house calls.

One night while on a house call . . . well, let me tell you first, my father was a longtime lawyer and was particularly anxious for me to be a success both professionally and financially. When we'd have dinner at the old family home out under the cottonwood trees in Los Griegos on North Rio Grande Boulevard, he'd ask what I'd done that day. I would say, "Aunt Mary had the flu, and I took care of her; Uncle Albert had a gallbladder attack after he ate an enormous salad with olive oil; brother John's little girl got her hand caught in the Mixmaster, and she had to have stitches . . ." He turned to me and said, "God almighty, you've worked all day and haven't made a cent!"

Another time he asked what I'd done, and I told him I'd been down in the South Valley seeing an old man who'd had a stroke. He lived in a tarpaper shack with his daughter, who was a dental hygienist. It was winter, and his bed was pulled up to the woodstove. One side of his face was very red, either from having had a stroke or from being too close to the fire. He couldn't swallow. So I went to Presbyterian and bought a couple of bottles of IV fluid from Dick, the old pharmacist, at five dollars a bottle. And the old lawyer said, "Are you going to get our money back?"

I said, "No, sir."

"Why did you do it then?" he asked.

"Because he couldn't swallow," I said. Well, Mother announced supper, and my father was very quiet.

The next day I got a call from Fred Luthy, president of Albuquerque National Bank, who had been closely associated with my father for forty years. Luthy had never seen the old gentleman under as much stress as when he told him about the old man who couldn't swallow. Luthy said that by the time my father had left the bank he had regained his composure and had set up a fund for patients who needed help and couldn't pay. Luthy also added that he and my father would check the account every month to make sure it was being handled properly.

Once, I went to see an elderly man in Martinez Town with severe pain from cancer in the jawbone. I noticed he had a red bandanna folded around his head, and underneath were a number of thin slices of cold potato next to his scalp. He told me that was a native remedy, but he was hurting very badly. He was beyond modern surgery and radiation therapy—this was before chemotherapy—but morphine and potato slices helped ease him out. Cases like these were the most enjoyable of all my practice.

Big Clouds and Blue Sky

Albuquerque's dry climate drew city dwellers in numbers. Lobo Theatre and the Monte Vista Fire Station looking northeast on Central. Photograph by Brooks Studio. Courtesy Albuquerque Museum. PA1978.151.589.

Freeways, Enchiladas, and the Corner Store

What Comes with Growth

Richard A. Bice grew up in Longmont, Colorado. He and his wife, Margaret, have lived in Albuquerque for sixty years. He is a retired engineer from the Los Alamos and Sandia National Laboratories. Aside from serving two terms on the City Commission, he helped establish the Museum of Natural History and the Albuquerque Museum. He is a charter member of the Albuquerque Archaeological Society and a trustee of the Archaeological Society of New Mexico. He has published more than twenty articles detailing his research on various Basket Maker, Pueblo, and Hispanic communities.

I am a westerner, having grown up in the small city of Longmont, Colorado. My wife, Margaret, and I were married soon after I received an engineering degree from Colorado A&M, now Colorado State University. I got an offer from Westinghouse Research Laboratories in Pittsburgh, Pennsylvania, where we moved. I conducted military research projects there during the early part of World War II. We wanted to get back west, and I was lucky enough to get an offer from

Richard A. Bice

Los Alamos Laboratories, and we moved in 1945. I participated in the design of the Fat Man atomic bomb, first tested at the Trinity Site in central New Mexico and later used to end World War II.

Soon enough, Albuquerque caught our attention, as we went there for shopping trips when gasoline rations would allow. At that time, the city had a population close to 45,000. At the end of 1946, major changes began to happen to this city. Because of the cold war, the nation's nuclear weapons program expanded rapidly, and a branch of the Los Alamos Labs called the Z Division was moved to Sandia Base. This branch was to carry out most of the engineering related to weapons development. We moved down from "the Hill," as Los Alamos was called back then, to help establish this infant branch. It grew into Sandia National Laboratories, with more than eight thousand employees, and I served as a vice

68

president for almost twenty years. Sandia and Kirtland eventually brought in more than twenty thousand new jobs.

Because there was no housing available in the city, we lived on the base for a few years. In 1949 we moved into the city proper. By 1953 Albuquerque had more than doubled in size and was approaching a population of 100,000. It faced a host of growth problems, many of which were associated with the city's inability to furnish adequate services in such areas as water, sewer, and street systems. The city operated under a form of government composed of a city manager and an elected five-person City Commission. However, over time the delegation of powers became somewhat blurred, particularly during the long tenure of Clyde Tingley, a charismatic commission chairman. Many citizens

Museum Planning
Richard Bice, Albuquerque Museum Board of Trustee, and Susanne de Borhegyi, Museum Director, view the model that would become the city's present museum. 1974. Courtesy Richard Bice.

were becoming concerned about the effectiveness of city government and ultimately in 1954 sponsored three candidates—a lawyer, a businessman, and an engineer—to run for commissioners. Well, I was the engineer! In the city election, we received an overwhelming vote and thus became the majority on the City Commission.

We addressed the city's need for operational and capital improvement monies, because the operating funds relied on property taxes and did not suffice. At that time the city budget was only about one million dollars, and it took us four months to find enough budget money to place a single, much-needed stoplight at a dangerous intersection. We convinced the state legislature to pass legislation allowing Albuquerque and other sizable cities in the state to impose a sales tax. It was an important cure for low capital improvement monies. When necessary, we changed the maturity dates of bonds from twenty years to five.

Another problem was the city's water utility. Severe water rationing was in place, and the supply did not keep up with demand. The system drew water from deep wells drilled into an aquifer that exists below the Rio Grande Valley. The aquifer was created millions of years ago by a major geologic discontinuity called a rift extending along the valley through Albuquerque, where water had collected. To cure the water crisis, new wells were drilled on the East Mesa to depths of a thousand feet or more. Similar wells were tried on the west side of the river, but they produced only hot mineralized water because of proximity to ancient volcanoes. But immediate cure was not enough. Because of the city's rapid growth, long-range planning was needed. Albuquerque is bounded on all sides by Indian land or Forest Service land, and it was estimated that within its boundaries, the city could reach a population of one million. It was clear that over time the groundwater would be depleted. As a supplemental source, we pledged to the federal government that the city would purchase water from the San Juan Diversion Project [southern Colorado and northern New Mexico waters], which would bring water from the west side of the Continental Divide and empty into the Chama River reservoirs north of Albuquerque, and from there channel into the city's water system. This project has been successful.

Another thing that needed attention was flood control, because during heavy rains, water originating in the mountains would rush down many arroyos and join with water from the streets and empty into the valley, whose floor is lower than the Rio Grande riverbed. This caused flooding in many homes in the summers of 1954 through 1956. I remember being called in the middle of the night by some poor souls who were flooded with water up to their knees. The solution was to improve the storm sewers, line the arroyos with concrete, and install intercepting north and south channels across the East Mesa to carry water into the river. Toward the end of my tenure, the problem of routing interstate freeways through the city came to a head. It included placement of the major I-40 and I-25 interchange. Fortunately, routes were available that minimized the destruction of community neighborhoods. When we first moved to Albuquerque, there were fifty miles of streets, and by 1962, at the end of my second term, there were six hundred miles, not including the newer freeways. Construction of smaller streets had not lagged either!

One particular highlight of my commission days was the city's 250th anniversary celebration. The Duke and Duchess of Alburquerque in Spain came as guests. The duke was a descendant of the man after whom our city is named. He and his wife charmed the city.

A few years after I left the commission, Pete Domenici and Harry Kinney were elected to its ranks. A new airport building, which had been authorized during my tenure, had just been completed, and the old airport, built by the WPA, was vacant. Harry Kinney asked me to head up an advisory committee to study the possibility of establishing a city museum in the old airport building. I happily took on the job, and within a few years the museum was created [in 1967], and the terminal building was remodeled to house it. Well, as time went on, the museum outgrew the space and needed a new permanent home. For its first twelve years, I chaired the Albuquerque Museum's Board of Trustees, and we were able to build and open a new museum at its present location near Old Town in 1979.

In the early 1980s, Governor Bruce King appointed me to a task force to study the status of fossils in the state. This was very appealing, since my interests in natural history had been fueled at an early age by family visits to the Denver Museum of Natural History. As a result of the task force, the New Mexico Museum of Natural History was created and built near the Albuquerque Museum.

Overall, there has never been a dull moment . . . always surprises and challenges.

Michael Gonzales was born on October 27, 1957, in Albuquerque. As a boy, he lived on Atlantic Street by the zoo. He played basketball at Albuquerque High, graduating in 1976. He has a business degree from the University of New Mexico. He and his family own and run Barelas Coffee House. Gonzales was active in the Barelas Neighborhood Association from 1985 to 2000 and served on the Barelas Merchants' Association Board of Directors from 1995 to 2000. Barelas is one of Albuquerque's oldest neighborhoods and is situated on the Camino Real, which witnessed early trade from Mexico during the 1600s.

My father had the building across Fourth Street that was vacant for several years. We [Michael and his brother Jim] were both kind of broke. I was a college student, and he was in between jobs, and we said, "Let's open a coffee house," and we did. My dad lent us his place, and that's the reason we have the Barelas

Michael Gonzales

No Reservations
Michael Gonzales (front row, right) at Barelas Coffee House, where it's first come, first served for regulars as well as newcomers. Courtesy Michael Gonzales.

Coffee House name. We just had coffee and pastries and sandwiches, and little by little we started adding to the menu. We were on that side of the street for seven years. We've been on this side for twenty. [The business] was something we thought we'd be in for a couple of years, just as extra income, but it just kept going! We didn't have any employees for the first eight months or so—we couldn't afford to pay anybody. Those first few months were the toughest. My dad had a grocery store right next door called Bromo's Grocery. He started it in the late thirties, and he was in business there for over fifty years. He passed away in 1991 and had it open until 1990. We grew up in the grocery store business, sweeping the floors, cleaning the windows, and stocking the shelves. My sister [Benita Villanueva] has been with us twenty-six years, and she's now one of the owners. My brother Jim sold his portion to her five years ago. He picked up our family recipes; they are my grandmother's chile recipes.

We've expanded over the years. We added an outside patio and purchased the building adjacent to us and made our production kitchen there. In 1991 we connected my dad's grocery store just north of us. We use it for storage. My dad told me that when he opened his grocery, Fourth Street stopped at the corner of Barelas and was just a dirt road. He said people would come to pick up their groceries in horse-drawn carts. His mother had a grocery store before he did—directly behind the restaurant. And her father is the one who started that business—probably in the late 1800s—so we're actually four generations in this neighborhood.

Dad's nickname was Bromo. His real name was Charles Borromeo —he was named after one of the saints. People thought he was nicknamed after Bromo Seltzer! But he helped us with the loan when we purchased this building. He was here until he passed away. He'd be here in the morning for his coffee, then at lunch for his bowl of chile, and then in the evening for the same thing.

The thing about this restaurant is that it has a lot of history. It was a restaurant known as Chano's back in the early thirties. The story on

Chano's is that the man who owned it had been in prison for killing somebody. I guess when he was in prison he learned how to cook, and when he got out he started his restaurant business. My dad said he was the hardest worker he had ever seen, because he'd be here at four in the morning cleaning trash cans and getting the business going, even though his business was all night, just dinner. He got out and sold to a business called Fito's. I remember coming in here with my dad when I was a little boy when it was Fito's. He had a piano in here, and he would play in the evening. They were in business until the early seventies, and then it started going downhill because there were not enough family members actively involved. So this place has been used as a restaurant for over seventy-five years. I found an old newspaper here with an advertisement from Chano's, and it had a four-digit telephone number!

It was quite a change for us moving from across the street, where we could seat only thirty people, to this. Back then, sometimes it would get so packed that my sister, who was the waitress, couldn't get to the tables, so some of the people would have to hand down the plates. Actually, when the business took off was when we added *menudo* . . . I'd never heard of it, never eaten it. But at that time, one of the people we hired mentioned that it was very popular with the Mexican clientele. We were probably serving as much menudo over there as we serve here.

Now we have our regulars, and have been told we're like the TV program *Cheers*. One regular came in twice a day for twenty-five years. He was like part of the family. We've had a lot of regular customers, from blue-collar to lawyers. The mayor [Martin Chavez] has a weekly meeting here. The previous mayor, Jim Baca, came in a lot, too. Bill Clinton came when he was governor and when he was running for president. We catered one of his gatherings, and though we couldn't get close, security told us he was eating a *chicharon* burrito before going on stage!

Barelas has seen a lot of change. Back when the railroad was here, it kept things going. When it closed down, it affected Barelas, since people had to move away [because there were no jobs], and the place became vacant. It was almost like a ghost town, with places boarded up. Now the community is almost like *the* place to be. There's talk of a fifty million-dollar project for a movie studio at the rail yard. Buildings are being shaped up. There's the old Red Ball Café down the street. It's been remodeled now. They used to serve little red chile burgers. When I was a kid, I'd go in and the ladies were Spanish speaking. They'd say, *"Cuántas?"* And I'd say about eight. In two bites they were gone.

Being able to stay in the same neighborhood where I grew up and having a business here is pretty nice. We don't want to expand. We serve 500 to 600 people a day, and on Saturdays it's 750. It's been hard work, but we're happy.

Finlay MacGillivray was born August 10, 1918, in Socorro. In the late 1880s, his father and uncles had come from Scotland and ranched in the Estancia area, where he learned to appreciate agricultural life. He came to Albuquerque in the early thirties. He managed the State Fair and served on the boards of the International Association of Fairs and Expositions and the Western Fairs Association. He also managed Ruidoso Downs and Sunland Park Racetrack.

I was the manager of the State Fair from 1963 to 1980. When I was appointed, I could see all sorts of potential in how to use the fairgrounds. With cooperation from all

Finlay MacGillivray

the different pueblos and Indian tribes, we built the Indian Village. The Indians did all their own building. Then we built the Spanish Village. The fair had lost some of its agricultural atmosphere, and I tried

Wilbur the Clown
One of the State Fair's cherished characters gives his boss a lift. Courtesy Finlay and Mollie MacGillivray.

to revive it. One fellow came in from his experimental farm in Farmington. He was winning all the prizes because he made his own exhibit; raised his own corn, squash, tomatoes, apples; and he worked with New Mexico State University crossing different products and using fertilizers to get fabulous produce. He was the center of attention and really enjoyed meeting people. I liked having him around to get people interested.

The fair was a separate entity from the state. We didn't get any support. In fact we made money, invested it, and improved on the grounds. When we made money at the fair, we put it to good use. We had one of the best-rated rodeos in the country. We were always in the top ten. We paid good purse money and drew good cowboys. We put on a good show.

We lived on the grounds [232 acres] for thirteen years in a trailer home. The fair was our life. Crows would fly up from the Rio Grande and cover the carnival grounds until it was black [Molly, his wife, adds]. The carnival people kept their animals on the grounds. They took care of their business pretty well. We saw the racetrack grow from nine to seventeen days of horse racing. The handle increased from four million to fourteen million dollars—"handle" money is what goes through the betting process. Most horses were Thoroughbreds, but we ran some quarter horse races. We introduced the Appaloosa race. We were able to give purse money large enough to draw out-of-state horses. Most were from New Mexico, but we got horses from Arizona, Colorado, and Texas.

There were some characters: Wilbur the Clown [who toyed with bulls to keep cowboys safe in the arena]. Outside the rodeo, he was a very religious person. In fact, he gave a sermon every Sunday morning when he was here. Then there was Fern Sawyer. She was on the fair's Board of Directors, and the way she rode a horse out in the arena . . . she had a lot to offer. She had long black hair that she wore up in a bun, and she would lead the Grand Entry every year.

We saw the fair grow but still keep its rural atmosphere. The FFA [Future Farmers of America] and 4-H kids got to stay on the fairgrounds with their livestock—all those kids brought in livestock hoping to win big money. We initiated a program where schools had their own State Fair Day. We saw attendance climb from a half a million to over a million in those years.

But now the fair has become more commercialized than it probably should be. They talk about moving it. I don't think it will move, or I hope not, for I feel it would be the beginning of the end of a good fair. There are different ideas as to where to put it—the West Mesa or south of the airport. I like it being in the heart of the city. That's contributed to its success—the availability.

Richard S. Martinez was born and raised in Las Vegas, New Mexico, and moved to Albuquerque when he was fourteen. He attended Lincoln Middle School and Albuquerque High School and joined the navy, where he served in the South Pacific. He and his wife, Clara, own and run Manuel's Market, named after its originator, Manuel Sanchez, Clara's father. Martinez helped organize the Citizen's Information Committee of Martinez Town in 1971 and has been active in the community's neighborhood association for over thirty years.

This store [Manuel's Market] is one of the only original buildings of Martinez Town [first plotted on an Albuquerque map in 1898] that is still here. It was built in 1924, and they dug out the basement and used the mud to make adobes and paid the laborers twenty-five cents for every one thousand adobes on the wall. Manuel Sanchez, my father-in-law, owned the store. I've been working in the store for sixty years. It's been a great experience seeing the neighborhood change. When I came on, we had a meat market and sold cold cuts. We were close to the railroad, and the bums heard by word of mouth that you could get free lunch here. Manuel served them bologna sandwiches with a Coke. He was always a kind person. He was a good friend of Clyde Tingley [city commissioner, state governor, and mayor of Albuquerque]. We used to do a landslide business for children. They'd come in and get two pieces of candy for a penny. Now kids come in with folding money.

Richard S. Martinez

Homes around here used to be of adobe without plumbing. In the seventies, the people of the community started wanting better housing. We were a blighted community because the city had zoned us as commercial, and we needed to be rezoned as residential. We had to fight. The old Longfellow School is a part of that story. St. Joseph Hospital said that if the school ever was to be changed, it had the first

The Voice of a Community
In the 1970s, Richard S. Martinez (front row, far right), with fellow Martinez Town citizens, called attention to the community's need to turn a blighted area into a safe one. Courtesy Richard S. Martinez.

option to buy the property. It wanted to put two medical towers on top of that berm. We went to the school board, and they said St. Joseph's claim was not binding. And we had some not-so-pleasant dealings with Sister Celeste and her staff. She was a poker player—first time I heard a nun cuss was when we took the letter protesting the sale of the property to the hospital. We got the school board to sympathize with us. The old school was condemned as unsafe; it had been built in 1937. Years later, when the engineers came in, they saw the cracks and deficiencies, and they decided to raze the school and build a new one.

We've been fighting City Hall and anyone who came along in order to keep our community intact. We had a protest march to City Hall from the Civic Auditorium. City Hall couldn't contain all the people in the march, so we had to come back up to the Civic Auditorium to hold a meeting . . . this was '75 or '76. There were about five hundred people who marched. They were the elderly, the community from Old Town, priests, even people from Barelas got involved. What we had going was that under the city's urban renewal program, they wanted to relocate everybody out of the community, build houses, then bring the people back in. What we decided was . . . well, we razed one house, put the lot up for sale so another person could buy it. When that person moved out of his house, it would be torn down and that lot sold to the next person. The process was repeated over and over. We had a lot of pro bono help from the University of New Mexico Architecture School. Now 95 percent of the people who lived here before, live here now. Some grandchildren are coming back to take over their grandparents' homes.

In this store, Manuel would have political meetings in the basement. He collected posters of a lot of the politicians who came through. He was a big Democrat. The last poster I got was from Lyndon Johnson. John Kerry came in when running for office. [Martinez points around the store at various posters.] There's Bill Richardson, President Kennedy, and Franklin Roosevelt. It's a lot more than a store [laughter]! It's still politics as usual. We're still working on our senior center. It was substandard in the late eighties, and we just now finished using the appropriated money for furniture and handicapped facilities. We put in a ceramics room, a commercial kitchen, and room for hairdressers and other services. So the fight goes on.

Robert Nordhaus was born in 1909, formed the law firm of Nordhaus and Moses (now Nordhaus, Haltom, Taylor, Taradash, and Bladh) in 1955, and retired in 1980. His specialty was water rights, oil, and gas law. He represented the Jicarilla Apaches, the Laguna Pueblo, and other Indian groups. He served on the Board of Directors of the Charles Ilfeld Company from 1945 to 1960, on the board and as board president of the Charles Ilfeld Hardware Company from 1960 to 1970, and as president of the Alvarado Realty Company from 1960 to 1976. He was chairman and president of the Sandia Peak Ski and Tram Companies from 1962 to 1976 and chairman emeritus thereafter. Nordhaus has been honored as one of sixteen Founders of Skiing USA and has been named a New Mexico Living Treasure. He retired from fly-fishing at age ninety.

My father was a merchant, and he came from Germany to Las Vegas, New Mexico, where he became president of Charles Ilfeld Company. We moved to Albuquerque in 1912, when I was three. Ilfeld built its warehouse at Twelfth and Central. We lived nearby. I went to Washington Junior High, Albuquerque High School, and my grades weren't so good, so I went to boarding school,

Robert Nordhaus

then to Yale and Yale Law School. I returned to Albuquerque in 1935.

A few friends and I started skiing in New Mexico in 1935. There were just a half dozen of us who would go up to the Sandia Mountains, where we made our own runs. We formed a club, the Albuquerque Ski Club, and we put in a rope tow. Well, back then we were practicing law, and we needed something else to do in the winter! So we drove up to the back of the mountain. There was nobody there, and we just started skiing. The Forest Service helped us clear the ski slope, and the club grew to about fifty people by 1936 or '37. Then I left to the war, where I was in the Tenth Mountain Division in Italy, and after the war I returned and formed a new company that bought out the Albuquerque Ski Club. Then we put in a 4,200-foot T-bar lift and extended

Skiing the Trees
The Sandia Mountains and their slopes have attracted people who love the outdoors for many years. 1940. Courtesy Albuquerque National Bank's Albuquerque Progress Collection, Albuquerque Museum. PA1980.61.289.

the ski area. In 1960 we started thinking about building a tram, and we extended the ski lifts to the top of the mountain. I had been in Europe and seen a lot of trams, and we figured this could be a good thing for Albuquerque in both summer and winter. We started as a little club, and now eight million passengers from all over the world will have ridden the tram by the end of 2005.

People are very outdoorsy here. There are fishermen, hunters, and a lot of skiers. Probably thousands of people have learned how to ski and have taken lessons here in the Sandias.

Thinking back, there were 14,000 people here in 1912, and the university was at the end of town. We had a cow and chickens at the house at Central and Twelfth streets. That didn't last too long! Now I still take the tram up for lunch. I can't ski anymore, but I go about once a week and look down at the city. It's amazing to see the growth.

Robert Stamm was born and raised in Albuquerque. He received degrees from the University of New Mexico and the U.S. Naval Academy. He claims to be 95 percent retired from Bradbury and Stamm Construction Company. He is a licensed engineer and was a land surveyor in New Mexico for more than forty-seven years. He has been a member of the New Mexico Commission on Higher Education and has received the UNM Regents' Recognition Medal, the Albuquerque Museum Foundation Award of Distinction, the Samaritan Counseling Center Ethics in Business Award, the UNM Zimmerman Award, the State of New Mexico Distinguished Public Service Award, and many more honors.

Albuquerque is the only place I've ever lived except for my time away in the navy in World War II. It's been a great place for me. I remember Supper Rock, an uplift of rocks near Juan Tabo in the far Northeast Heights. We would get in a wagon with blankets and go out on hayrides and have picnics. It was a big spring event. Now that I think of it, the place wasn't that big, really, maybe fifty yards by fifty yards. We thought it was pretty far out, and now it's in the middle of a residential area! I would go with dates. Flor [his wife, Florence Brad-

Robert Stamm

bury] and I had our first date and went to the east side of the mountains. We skied on the road back in 1936. A lot of our dates were spent skiing. It was fun being part of the beginning of skiing then.

My dad [Roy Stamm] was a man ahead of his time. He rode in a balloon over the mountains long before hot-air ballooning got popular. He wrote books on fly-fishing. Near Tenth Street and Central there's a little street called Kent, where he built an outdoor recreation place called Stamm's. It had an outdoor nickelodeon, a dance floor, and he rented bicycles. He sold skis and hunting and fishing stuff, had badminton courts, Ping-Pong tables, and the first and only lawn tennis court in New Mexico. I played a lot of tennis in that time. It was

Boating Down the Rio Grande
Robert and Florrie Stamm watch one of their favorite city events as people race whatever can float through the river's highs and lows. Courtesy Robert and Florence Stamm.

before the war, maybe 1940. He just liked young people and the outdoors. He was a strong proponent of anything outdoors. He got me started in tennis, fly-fishing, and skiing. I won three state tennis high school championships. I was a shy kid and sports was good for me. Stamm's was a great spot for kids, but it just didn't make any money. And when the war started, it went out of business.

Florrie's dad [O. G. Bradbury] built Kirtland Air Force Base right before the war, as well as other bases around the state. When I came back from the war, I began working for her dad in 1946 and am still on the payroll! In 1957 the business became Bradbury and Stamm. Then in 1979 we sold it, and it is being carried on as a private company. Her dad built the old Albuquerque High School gym in 1938, and my class was the first to graduate in it. Then a few years later, we rebuilt the high school . . . that was rewarding. We built the Albuquerque Biolog-ical Park. I'm very pleased with that. Then we did the Genoveva Chavez recreational facility in Santa Fe and the gym for the commu-nity college. We did the Fine Arts Center at the College of Santa Fe and refurbished the castle at the United World College in Las Vegas. Working with Armand Hammer was very fun . . . with someone of that stature. But those are things around the state.

A big part of my life here has been in volunteer time . . . hours and hours stretching back forty-five years. In the late fifties or early sixties, I got involved in the United Way, and I saw how much good we could do and wanted to be a part of it. I've worked with the Albuquerque Community Foundation to help raise money and am a trustee at the Albuquerque Museum . . . we built the recent addition. Most exciting was working on New Mexico's Board of Higher Education for nine years under four governors. Education is critical to the quality of life here. I enjoy the volunteer life. To me, that means so much.

Shaping the Place
The Rio Grande flows through the city's oldest quadrants.
In its winding, it touches the imaginations and lives of
many people. Circa 1975. Photograph by Anthony Anella.

Mud, Water, Wool, and Meem

Environmental, Historic, and Cultural Preservation

Anthony Anella was born on January 23, 1956, in Albuquerque, where he grew up. He is the principal of Anthony Anella Architect AIA, an award-winning practice dedicated to site-sensitive design, and a partner in Conservation Design Partners, an Albuquerque-based group that specializes in conservation-based design and development. He is also a member of the board of the New Mexico Land Conservancy. He has coauthored two books: Never Say Goodbye: The Albuquerque Rephotographic Survey Project *and* Saving the Ranch: Conservation Easement Design in the American West.

Albuquerque is a fundamental part of who I am. When I went away to college on the East Coast and I would meet people for the first time, after introducing myself, the next thing I would say was that I was from Albuquerque. Place is important to me, and this is my place.

In college I organized a kayak expedition down the length of the Rio Grande as a way of focusing my academic studies and also as a way of getting a little closer to home. Two books inspired the trip: one was author Paul Horgan's *Great River: The Rio Grande in North American History,* and the other was photographer Laura Gilpin's *Rio Grande, River of Destiny.* I was fortunate to meet both authors. Dartmouth College sponsored the trip, and the National Geographic Society provided the photographic equipment, processing, and film. We averaged a little less than twenty miles a day, and I will never forget the feeling of kayaking into the Gulf of Mexico after going 1,888 miles from source to sea.

We started in April 1977, where the Rio Grande begins at Stony Pass at the Continental Divide above Creede, Colorado. It was a low snowfall year, and the lack of water was part of the story from the very beginning. In the San Luis Valley of Colorado, water was diverted from the river into irrigation ditches every few miles. At one point the only river we could find was an irrigation ditch, so we put our boats in

In His Bones
*Tony Anella blends
Albuquerque's older
architectural styles
into contemporary
homes and buildings in
order to conserve the
feel that makes the city
a place he never wants
to leave. Courtesy
Anthony Anella.*

there! Just above Alamosa, Colorado, the water ran dry. They had irri-
gated the river out. So we borrowed bicycles from Adams State College and rode to the Lobatos Bridge at the Colorado and New Mexico
state line . . . this is where Colorado diverts water back into the river
for New Mexico and Texas in accordance with the 1939 Rio Grande
Compact. Enough water was diverted back into the river from the irrigation ditches that we could use our kayaks. We went through the
upper box, which was incredibly treacherous. There were places where
the water just disappeared into a sieve of boulders.

We had enough water to make it to Albuquerque, where we had to
put our boats in the clear ditch—the ditch that diverts water from the
river in Algodones [on the Rio Grande north of Albuquerque] and
runs parallel to the river through Albuquerque. We floated through
the city in the clear ditch and had to portage Route 66 at the Central
Avenue Bridge! When coming through Albuquerque, Maxie Anderson took us up in a balloon, and we got some great river shots from the
air. At the upper end of Elephant Butte, the river was nothing but silt.
We were lucky we didn't drown in the mud. Below El Paso, the river
dries up completely, so we rode bicycles down to Presidio-Ojinaga

and the confluence of the Rio Conchos, which comes up from Mexico. From there we had water all the way to the Gulf of Mexico. When we were about four hundred miles away from the Gulf of Mexico, we began to smell the sea salt in the air. It was incredibly exciting to finally kayak into the gulf after traveling for that long.

Twenty-five years later, I wanted to show my family the river the way I know it. So I designed a sculpture based on the experience. I call it *Hydrograph* because it monitors the changing water level of the river. It includes stones that my family and I have gathered all along the river. My children have seen where the river begins and where it used to flow into the Gulf of Mexico. The sculpture is part of Albuquerque's Public Art Program and is on display at the Explora Science Center and Children's Museum. This river and this town are part of my soul. They inspire my work.

Lisa Dickens Madsen Maurer *was born February 11, 1947, in Fair-banks, Alaska. She moved to Albuquerque when she was five and a half months old. She attended Valley High School and Fort Lewis College, where she received a degree in American history, and the University of New Mexico, where she earned her master's. She is executive director of the Public Lands Interpretive Association, formerly the Southwest Natural and Cultural History Association. Her honors include a Partners in Excellence Award from the Bureau of Land Management and the U.S. Forest Service.*

I was working at Burnt Wood Leather Shop in Old Town, selling sandals, when in 1977 I had a chance to go on a dory trip on the Colorado River. I left my job to take that trip, and it changed my life completely. I had never understood these vast lands, though I grew up in Albuquerque. Very ironically, it's been my husband, Stephen Maurer, who is Hungarian, who has instilled the whole appreciation of our country's public lands in me.

Lisa Madsen Maurer

I became absolutely hooked and passionate about what not-for-profit organizations do to educate people about public land in the United States. I've been doing this [coordinating public land use] for almost twenty-four years now. In the beginning [1981], our entire business [Public Lands Interpretive Association] focused on the migration of

A Dirt Road
In the late 1950s, Rio Grande Boulevard was just a dirt road cutting by alfalfa fields and a few homes. Lisa Dickens Madsen Maurer grew up in one of those homes. Courtesy Lisa Dickens Madsen Maurer.

birds in New Mexico and Texas. Now we sell maps, operate book-stores and campgrounds, and produce a vibrant Web site on public lands west of the Mississippi, no matter who manages them, be it the Bureau of Land Management, U.S. Forest Service, U.S. Fish and Wildlife, or any agency. We have a lending library here in Albu-querque with a couple thousand books on the shelves. We serve hunters, off-road-vehicle enthusiasts, fishermen and -women, hikers, campers. I like to think in some little way we have worked to create a resource here that is unparalleled in the world.

In 1999 we organized the American Frontiers Project, where for sixty days two teams of people, one in Columbus, New Mexico, and the other in Glacier National Park, trekked toward one another on public land. They hiked, rode horseback, canoed, and rafted; they used all-terrain vehicles and mountain bikes. The National Geo-graphic Alliance was involved, along with Honda Motor Corporation, Coleman, and the list goes on and on. They hiked 3,200 miles all together and met in the Wasatch-Cache National Forest in Utah. We [as a country] want to take a good look at what we have in all these lands, for there might be a time when we don't have such luxury.

I think my experiences as a child growing up here in the fifties and sixties helped inspire my work today. I just remember freedom. The North Valley was sparsely populated, and when I was ten to twelve, I'd be gone all day. I'd hear my mother calling us for lunch, and we'd come in, only to leave again. We spent way more time outside than inside. We'd wander around and sometimes take picnics. Rio Grande Boulevard was dirt back then. Milk and bread were still delivered by trucks to our home. I feel so old! As a child, I remember feeling that everyone was in the same boat, whether you were Hispanic, Indian, or Anglo. It never occurred to me that we were different.

The way Albuquerque has grown and changed . . . I tell people it's as if I've moved three or four times, because the city seems different while all along I've been here! Kids now won't have the same experi-ence we were able to have, and we want to instill in them an appreciation for what is here. We have the river and the mountains. The geography of a place makes you reflect on who you are in connection to it. I can't think of any other place that has this feel.

Now we work in tandem with the Open Space Coalition of Albuquerque. There are tours given in spring and fall, starting at the west side volcanoes and going to parks in the city and all the way to Elena Gallegos Park in the Sandia foothills. We are told that we're Albuquerque's best-kept secret, and I believe we are.

Ray Powell was born in Albuquerque and grew up here. He attended the University of New Mexico, where he received his undergraduate degree in biology and anthropology and his master's degree in botany. He received his veterinary medical degree from Tufts University. Powell is former executive director of the Valles Caldera National Preserve in the Jemez Mountains. A practicing veterinarian, he currently is chairman of the state veterinary board. During his decade tenure as elected state land commissioner, he established the twenty-square-mile Mesa del Sol master-planned community and La Semilla Nature Preserve in Albuquerque. The beneficiaries of this multibillion-dollar project are the public schools and the University of New Mexico.

I was born in Albuquerque. My parents were part of the Manhattan Project [the weapons and defense program at Los Alamos National Laboratories during World War II]. My mom was a physicist, and my dad was an engineer. He helped start Sandia Labs and spent his career there. Our home was on the edge of the university, and I remember Lomas getting paved! There was mesa all around us, with maybe a few little outcrops of buildings or homes, and the University of New Mexico was our playground.

Ray Powell

I was fifteen when we moved down to the North Valley and I went to Valley High School. It was just wonderful. We had all sorts of animals that I loved; it was like Noah's ark. I loved being outside and riding horses and taking care of family animals and especially my dogs. Oh, we ran on the ditches with absolute impunity. I've gone through a couple of guardian angels to get me out of a few things. I think they are in nursing homes now!

The best thing was being outside to connect with the natural world. I was watching a CNN news account that the average time an average teenager spends out-of-doors is thirty minutes a day. I'm trying to get kids to learn to empathize with something other than themselves. In

Outside in Albuquerque
*Ray Powell, a devoted outdoors enthusiast, promotes the healthy life
through enjoyment of the city's parks and preserves. Courtesy Ray Powell.*

my veterinary practice, I'd see animals with real signs of abuse . . .
they were being victimized by cigarette burns or whatever, and I'd
look at the person with the animal and see in his or her face the same
thing. I started to see a manifestation of abuse . . . no matter if it had
four legs, two legs, was a bird, or what. The abuse comes from a total
lack of connection with the natural world. Our sense of wonder can
get crushed if we are not outside, and it gets replaced with anger and
frustration. How are we going to feel anything if we are running from
cars to air-conditioned homes or offices?

The bosque used to be thick with trees until lately. We've had wild-
fires, and now we have more open space. I think that's been good . . .
the fires were viewed as catastrophic, when really it was part of a natural order. We're pulling in more migratory birds. I even saw a blue
heron in my backyard the other day. I live in the house I grew up in,
and the trees and grapevines we planted when I was a kid are mature.
We have three and a half acres and are converting those from high to

low water use. Water is such a contentious thing here. I want to conserve it.

C. S. Lewis said that what we call man's power over nature turns out to be a power exercised by some men over other men with nature as its element. If we wreck this whole place [Albuquerque], we become like every other place. We're just now starting to leave a lighter footprint on the land here. Albuquerque in its day was like the wild Old West. It was boom or bust. But now, the way we will make it as a community is to ask ourselves, how do we preserve this place so that we can enjoy it? I think that is a very important question.

Penny Rembe was born in Dallas and met her husband, Armin Rembe, at the world's fair in Seattle. They moved to Albuquerque in 1967 and have never left. She served on the Board of Regents at the University of New Mexico and has been active in city planning and cultural preservation for many years. She has served on the Board of Directors of the North Valley Neighborhood Association, Albuquerque Friends of Art, and the Anderson Schools of Management at the University of New Mexico. She has owned a gift store, a deli, and a catering business and has served as a trustee for the village of Los Ranchos de Albuquerque.

My husband, Armin, was here from Seattle on a medical fellowship in oncology at the University of New Mexico in 1967, and after three months he said, "Go look for a house, I'm never moving." I kept driving by the old Lovelace house behind the Lovelace clinic on Ridgecrest Drive. It was a John Gaw Meem house, built in the forties. Well, it came up for sale, and Dr. Lovelace's daughters sold it to us and left a lot of the furniture in the house. We lived with the clock or piano, and year after year the daughters would come and pick up something. The kitchen was an old industrial kitchen, and we called John Gaw Meem to redesign it. He said he was too old, but to call George Pearl, who influenced us greatly and introduced us to the different aspects of preserving cultural heritage. It was a charming house built around a

Penny Rembe

Living History
Penny Rembe keeps the past alive at Los Poblanos Inn and La Quinta Cultural Center, where she tends organic gardens and lavender fields. Courtesy Penny Rembe.

courtyard, with a guesthouse where all the astronauts of the time stayed when they came to Lovelace Hospital for physicals. They left their signatures on the door.

We lived in the house for ten years and then bought what is now Los Poblanos Inn and La Quinta Cultural Center, once the family estate of Ruth and Albert Simms [former U.S. congressional representatives]. Albert Simms's nephew, also named Albert Simms [discussed in the "Treasure" chapter], and his wife, Barbara, were living in it at the time. We heard they wanted to sell. I thought they wanted someone to carry on the tradition. So Armin's sister and her husband bought La Quinta, and we bought Los Poblanos. While we were doing work on the property, we found a [fourteenth-century] Indian site, and it turned into an archaeological dig for a while. Previously, the land was owned by the Armijo family as a ranch. People would come by all the time to tell us what they had done when they had worked there, and we understood the importance of what the Simmses had created. Ruth Hanna Simms built La Quinta in 1937 to be a work of art and a cultural center. John Gaw Meem designed it. Thornton Wilder read here; the June Music Festival started here. Peter Hurd [a famous New Mexico painter] painted a mural; the doors were carved by Gustave Baumann [another famous New Mexican artist].

Well, after twenty years, my in-laws, the Walkers, decided they wanted to move, and I started calling people about buying the house. Well, no one wanted a 15,000-square-foot house! At that point, we went into gear to try to buy them out and put the two properties together again and open it up to the community. Instead of selling the land to development, we put some of it into agricultural trust, where we now grow lavender and organic produce. We turned the house into an inn and run La Quinta as a cultural center, where we hold conferences. It's listed on both the State and National Register of Historic Places. We're trying to show people that you don't have to sell your land to keep it going [economically]. Because of the organic farming, we have farmers coming here from around the country [to discuss growing techniques]. Agritourism is big now, and people come here for our lavender products.

One thing that was important to us when we came to Albuquerque was that the city was small enough that we could be out and feel like we were part of the community, and nothing was so fancy you couldn't join it. That's what I love about this place. It isn't that fancy or too formal to put you off.

Pearl Sunrise was born and raised in a family of thirteen children at Whitewater, New Mexico, on the Navajo reservation south of Gallup. She attended Fort Wingate Boarding School for her elementary and high school education and received her bachelor's and master's degrees from the University of New Mexico. Sunrise is a professor at the Institute of American Indian Arts in Santa Fe. She has traveled to New Zealand on a Fulbright Scholarship, and other awards have taken her to South Africa, Canada, and France. Her honors include the Governor's Award for Outstanding New Mexico Woman and the Great Achievement Award, State Fair Indian Village.

I was asked to demonstrate the processes of Navajo weaving at the State Fair [in 1974], and I have been educating people since then on picking wool, pulling it apart, then carding wool, spinning and dyeing wool, to warping on the loom, to finally the weaving. People from all walks of life have come to watch. There were some people who would come every day during the fair while I wove my rug. Sometimes they would buy it. Schoolkids came from many schools, and if the kids came from Navajo Reservation, I would present the process of weaving in Navajo so they would learn in their native tongue.

Pearl Sunrise

Initially I was demonstrating in a tiny one-room hut, and when my husband, an architect, planned the new Indian Village, he did it so it would better reflect our culture. He worked with the State Fair Commission on this. We changed the dance area from being a concrete circle to a large area on the ground. In the last few years, I've been demonstrating weaving in the Navajo Hogan [a traditional Navajo structure made of logs and mud, with a roof of mud], much like the hogan I was born and raised in during childhood years. I love the time at the fair because of the aromas of fry bread, fresh-baked oven breads and pies, lamb stews, and lamb sandwiches grilled over hot coals.

The Fine Art of the Loom
Pearl Sunrise grew up weaving and continues to share her knowledge each year at the State Fair. Collectors have been know to purchase her demonstration rugs while still on the loom. A typical rug will require several months to complete. Courtesy Pearl Sunrise.

My own children have been a part of my life as I weave. I have three daughters. They would come to the fair each year. One daughter was

Miss Indian New Mexico. I was so excited when I heard the announcement—my friends thought I did a somersault!

In the early years, my uncle did his sand painting while I wove. One time, he was creating his sand painting in the hogan when this tall woman and her friend came storming in looking for the sand painting. She was looking up, because she thought he was doing it on the ceiling or wall, and asked, "Where is the sand painting?" My uncle looked up and said, "Lady, you're standing on it!" Well she got all red and apologized, then left. We laughed at that!

One time I was weaving a four-by-six-foot storm pattern, a style of my own, when this tall, good-looking Navajo man came in with his friend. "There she is," he said in a loud voice. "The woman I've been looking for." Now I just kept on weaving, and he said, "I have four bulls, four horses, two concho belts [intricately detailed belts decorated with flat silver disks], and about ten head of sheep that I can give as dowry." My brother-in-law was standing in the corner just grinning. Bill, my husband, always said I wasn't worth anything! Men came in many times and were proposing in roundabout ways.

My uncle always signs me up with his dance group as a Navajo feather dancer or a Navajo squaw dancer or as a Yei-Bi-Cheii dancer. So I've educated people on tribal dances and songs along with weaving. I'm not a competitive person, but one year my relative enlisted me to perform as a soloist in the Navajo song and dance event. They came running into the hogan where I was weaving and pinned a number on me and grabbed my Navajo moccasins called wraparounds—a whole deerskin for each leg—and my concho belt hanging on the wall. By that time, they called my number, and I sang two Navajo songs I had learned from my dad when I was a little girl herding sheep. Later, I won first place. It's hard for me to believe I won because I grew up where everyone shared and was equal. This was special for me.

I feel comfortable in the Indian Village at the State Fair because it makes me feel connected to my ancestry and culture. I learned to weave when I was seven or eight. My mother and my grandmothers were weavers. I just emulated what they did. I didn't learn in lessons, but just by doing. Every year I get a visit from Navajo women who want to learn to weave. We have a conversation, then they go home with instructions. Then the next year they come back wanting to learn another technique.

Last year I got a very special visit from a 105-year-old Navajo grandmother, who came in a wheelchair. I spoke to her in the Navajo language. She told her grandchildren, "She speaks my language, even in weaving . . . Now go get lost!" She sat next to me and told me stories about how she was a good weaver. She touched my hands and my fingers. She stayed until nightfall, and then her grandchildren took her home. It was quite a blessing.

A Penny for Your Thoughts

The Contemplative Side

One Man's Shrine, 1993
Horacio Martinez in Santa Barbara and the Martinez Town neighborhood, northeast of downtown. With its Hispanic inhabitants and closely knit adobe homes, the community is akin to many northern New Mexican villages. Photograph by Miguel Gandert.

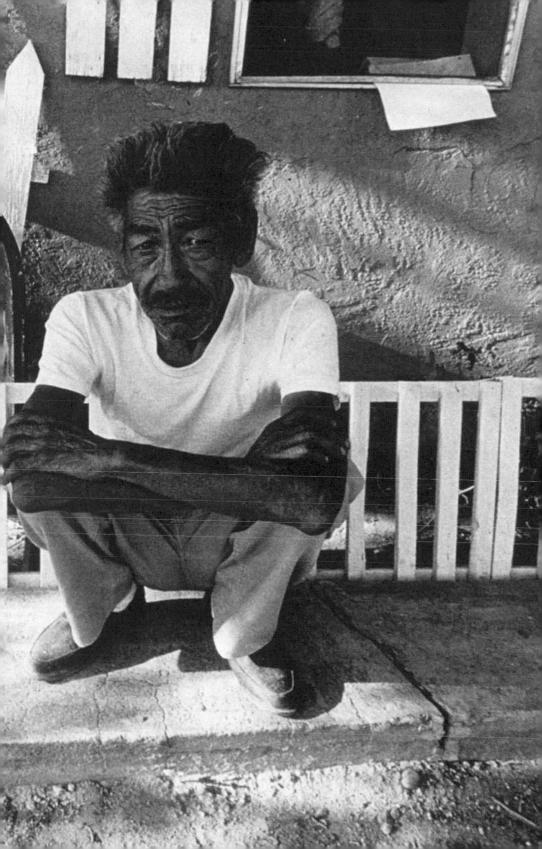

Jacqueline J. Baca was born and raised in Albuquerque. She has been president of Bueno Foods since 1986. She started work in the plant there, on the production line, at age sixteen. She holds a bachelor's degree in political science and a master's degree in business administration from the University of New Mexico. In 1998 the Association of Women in Communications gave her and Bueno Foods the Vanguard Award for supporting women in the workplace. In 1997 Baca was the first Hispanic woman accepted into UNM's Robert O. Anderson Schools of Management, and the U.S. Hispano Chamber of Commerce named her Businesswoman of the Year in 1994. She has served on the board of the Barelas Community Development Corporation and currently sits on the Wells Fargo Community Advisory Board and on the New Mexico Community Capital Board of Directors.

Our company is rooted in family and tradition. The essence of the business really emerged when my dad and his siblings were growing up in an agricultural setting in the South Valley of Albuquerque. My dad was the last to be born in Barelas. My grandparents decided to move their large family to Five Points [a South Valley neighborhood where five streets intersect],

Jacqueline J. Baca

where they had some land. My Grandpa Refujio worked for the Atchison, Topeka and Santa Fe Railway all his life, but when he would come home, he would go to work in his garden until sundown, dreaming about one day owning his own business. They grew fruits and vegetables and lots of chile. My Grandma Filomena was a wonderful cook, and they grew up eating very well. I think that was the way she nurtured her kids. When there was an overabundance, my dad and two of his brothers would go around the community, up and down Fourth Street downtown, with pails of produce to sell.

After serving in World War II, my dad and his brothers came back to Albuquerque but had a difficult time finding jobs. They went to school on the GI Bill at St. Joseph when it was still Catholic Teachers' College on Indian School Road. That's where my dad met my mom. My dad started teaching. But unlike my mom, who was a teacher and counselor for thirty years in Albuquerque Public Schools, it wasn't for him, and he lasted six weeks! Meanwhile, in 1946, my Grandpa Refujio remortgaged his house and encouraged several of his sons, including my dad, to scrape money together to buy a grocery store on Bridge in Five Points. They called it the Ace. My grandfather's dream was coming true. He told his sons to be in charge of their own destinies and to make their own opportunities, as well as opportunities for others in the community.

Soon, the Safeways and the Piggly Wigglys began displacing the mom-and-pop stores. My dad and his brothers could see the writing on the wall. They realized that to survive, they had to take their business in another direction. At that time, they cooked up their lunches

in the store, and people would come in and comment about how good it smelled. The customers would ask, "Why don't you sell us some of that food?" And so they started a carryout from the grocery store, featuring my grandmother's home-cooked recipes.

One Sunday evening in September, my dad and his brothers were sitting around the supper

Grand Opening, 1984
Jacqueline Baca and her father, Joseph, celebrate a new start as Bueno Foods opens a chile processing plant and operations site in the Barelas neighborhood. Courtesy Bueno Foods.

table with their parents, just throwing out ideas about how to grow their business. It was the 1950s, and freezers were becoming popular. Birdseye frozen vegetables were coming into their own. According to my dad, his sister scooped up the last bit of chile and said, "Wouldn't it be nice to eat roasted chile all year?" My dad said that everyone was quiet for the longest time.

After that, they started flame roasting and freezing green chile . . . they invented the process really. They developed equipment because there was nothing out there to roast chile with on a large scale. I don't have a sense of how much chile they processed then, but they did contract out to buy chile from farmers in southern New Mexico all along the Rio Grande basin. Today we still buy chile from some of those same farmers; it's in the second generation now.

When I think of Albuquerque, I think of Albuquerque in the autumn and that aroma of freshly roasted green chile. Fall was a bittersweet time for us kids because it meant the beginning of the chile harvest, and it meant my dad would work many long hard hours. But when the green chile harvest began in mid-August, my dad would bring home a little of the fresh chile from the first day of processing. My mom would roast it up and make *chile picado*. She would chop it up and put in garlic and fresh tomato from our garden . . . my mom didn't grow up with fresh tomato in the chile, but my dad had. I still remember my mom making homemade tortillas on her grandmother's *comal* and what they would call cube steak, a cheaper cut of meat, which she would pound until it was tender. We would eat the meat wrapped in tortillas and fresh green chile for supper. It was our annual tradition at the start of green chile season.

It's really our dream now to celebrate our heritage and to share our traditional family recipes and authentic food with people not only in our state but all over—worldwide. We've had restaurants in the Cayman Islands and England that buy our product. There's also a store in Maui that sells our salsa and natural food stores in Canada that sell our tortillas. Here, we are so lucky to have such a rich cultural heritage. Our food defines us, makes us unique, I think, and it's a privilege to be able to have a role in preserving that part of our culture.

I always wondered where the name "Bueno" came from. My aunt swore that my dad and his brothers used to be called "the good boys," and lots of girls in Barelas wanted to marry them because their mother was religious and industrious and their father was optimistic and generous. Knowing my grandparents, I know it must have been true!

Conroy Chino grew up at Acoma Pueblo and has lived in Albuquerque for more than thirty years. He was appointed cabinet secretary for the New Mexico Department of Labor on January 1, 2003, and has worked in Albuquerque's broadcast news business since 1978. He received a bachelor of arts degree from the University of New Mexico, did graduate work at Princeton University, and was awarded a Nieman Fellowship at Harvard University. His honors include the Investigative Reporters and Editors National Award for Excellence in Investigative Reporting, the Rocky Mountain Emmy Award for Best Investigative Reporting, and a Peabody Award for Outstanding Documentary for Surviving Columbus.

When I was ten or eleven, my parents brought my family to the State Fair. They loaded all of us into a pickup truck, and we left the reservation [Acoma Pueblo] to head east. I was mesmerized by the city and even more so by the State Fair. What stands out in my mind is going to McDonald's for the first time. There was one near the fairgrounds, and I remember experiencing a McDonald's hamburger. I think I liked it!

Conroy Chino

At the fair, I remember being swept away by the sights, sounds, and smells. There were so many people . . . the lights on the Ferris wheel and the carneys . . . the games, the rides. We went to the barn area, where they were selling animals, and my folks bought a rabbit. We named it Fair Lady. We took her home and put her in a box. The next day we went off to school. Well, Fair Lady got out of the box, and we had a huge cat that didn't appreciate a rabbit running around the house and attacked it. Fair Lady died of fright under my bed.

Over the years, we would come to Albuquerque to shop and go to the State Fair in the fall. But I didn't come here to stay until I was a student at UNM in the late sixties. My life was pretty restricted to the campus. It gave me a chance to meet students, not only from other

From Investigative Reporter to Secretary of Labor
Conroy Chino balances life by returning to his home at Acoma Pueblo on weekends.
Photograph by Daryl Black.

tribes around the state but from around the country. It was a time of change and tumultuousness, with the civil rights movement and protests against the Vietnam War. I was exposed to a lot of different ideas, and I started to question the values I had grown up with at the reservation. For many young people of my generation who grew up on the reservation, there was . . . well . . . a lot of it was brainwashing. We were made to believe that somehow being Native was not as good as being white. That was ingrained and reinforced through schools, through books, textbooks, and television. We were one of the first families to have a TV set, and we'd spend the afternoons on Saturdays watching these grade-B westerns of Indians getting shot and killed, and it perpetuated a lot of stereotypes in me. So by the time I got to UNM and met other people who were exposed to the ideas being propelled by the civil rights movement, I started questioning, while trying to find myself. The whole identity issue rose to the top for a lot of

Native students, and we got swept up by all the activism that was going on at that time with the blacks and the Hispanics or, at that time, the Chicanos. We were partnering with them to raise the awareness, or consciousness, not only in our own immediate communities but in the federal government. We were idealistic and romantic. I was involved in a lot of that—the student protests, the sit-ins at the Bureau of Indian Affairs, the demonstrations. I think it really allowed me the chance to grow. I'd go back to the reservation and tell my grandparents that it was okay to be an Indian. They would laugh and say, "Well, when did you stop [thinking it was okay]?"

I had to come all the way to Albuquerque to learn about myself and to appreciate what I had back on the reservation—the culture, the belief system, the philosophy, the tribal outlook on everything in life, from the environment to the religious side to the songs and the chants, the ritual. The thing that stands out about Albuquerque for me is that I had to come sixty miles off my reservation to discover my tribe.

I fell in love in Albuquerque and had a son, developed friendships, got introduced to the world of broadcasting while I was at UNM. I was the first Native American host for a program called *Singing Wire*. I think it was that stint in radio that helped me get into television news. Then I graduated and left to go to Princeton. When I started looking for work, it was here in Albuquerque where an opportunity arose to work in a radio station. I worked for KQEO, rewriting wire copy for Ed Pennybacker, who did news at the top of the hour and bottom of the hour. I went from there to another radio station, KDEF. Then one day I went by Channel 7 to inquire for a job. Dick Knipfing, this institution, actually hired me. I had no experience in television news. I had never picked up a microphone. I got the job working weekends. The rest is history, as they say. Twenty-five years later, and Dick Knipfing is still around . . . he was the one and only anchor in my life. I credit him for giving me the chance to build a career, especially for someone who had never taken a journalism class in his entire life. I think about all those years of covering Albuquerque, both as a general assignment reporter, then as an investigative reporter, and exposing a lot of Albuquerque's deep dark secrets, chasing after crooks, corrupt politicians, policemen, and pedophile priests. It was all done with the idea of trying to right wrongs, with the basic tenet of informing Albuquerque's viewing audience in such a way that they could make an informed decision.

While all this was going on professionally, I never lost sight of my tribe. My wife is from Acoma, and we make a trek back once a week. We try to maintain our ties to our pueblo. We still participate in religious activity there, the dances, and the ritual. We still speak the language. We have strong family ties and clan ties. It's been a real balancing act for me—living my life in Albuquerque, and still, after all these years, decades, we talk about Acoma as being our home.

Blair Darnell was born in New Orleans on December 28, 1922. She has lived in Albuquerque for over fifty years, most of that time on her and her late husband Casey's horse property west of the Rio Grande. She is a director emeritus of the American Quarter Horse Association and an advisory board member of the Alfonso Ortiz Center for Intercultural Affairs.

When I drove here from North Carolina in 1952, I had my dog and everything important to me packed into my station wagon. I spent four nights on the road, and on the last night I was in a community east of Albuquerque. There was a big sign that said, "Last Stop Motel," and I took them for their word and stayed there. I had to get to the University of New Mexico the next day; I had transferred from Middlebury College. Well, I got up early and drove through Tijeras Canyon. There was a yellowish glow. I got out of my car and looked down from the mountain pass to the desert below. It was just gorgeous with the sun rising. I went on to enroll at the university in Latin American studies and Spanish, though later in life I wish I would have chosen anthropology, for I love it. That year I went to an event involving the Sheriff's Posse [a group of horsemen and -women from the Bernalillo Sheriff's Department who take part in parades, rodeos, and other horse-related activities], and I happened to meet a person named Casey Darnell. I told him I wanted a

Blair Darnell

A Life with Horses
For more than forty years, Blair Darnell has inspired children and adults to discover the joys of horse-manship. Courtesy Albuquerque Magazine, 2005.

horse. I'm not sure why I said that—mostly it was just something to say. So one day this guy shows up at my house with a sorrel that was pretty scrawny looking. I had a saddle, and he gave me a bridle and off he drove. Well, the horse threw me, but eventually we got acquainted. I didn't see Casey for a while. Then we met again one night and went dancing and to some rodeos. A few years later we got married.

Our life has been in horses since 1955. Casey trained, and I was a good feeder and waterer. I had a daughter, and Casey had two sons. We had three children together. We had almost as much fun with the kids as with the horses [laughter]! There was always something happening with those kids. Anyway, Casey and I both took part in organizations that represented horses. He was involved in racing. He had a lot of respect behind the barns at the track. He always had good help. He did compete in reining . . . there was Joe Lauro, a great quarter horse, and Miss Fortune, an incredibly good dogging horse. I didn't show much. I became involved in the Rio Grande Horse Association, which was instrumental in building the growth of horse ownership here in the North Valley and South Valley. We were both involved in local 4-H clubs. I suspect an average of two thousand horses have been through our stables—the ones we trained and managed. Some went on to become champions. We gave a lot of lessons, and some people have gone on to be masters of Casey's horsemanship techniques.

I loved riding the ditch and the river. One of my fondest memories was organizing rides for the 4-H kids. A few times, Casey took a bunch of kids and their horses through Corrales up into what has become Rio Rancho toward Laguna Pueblo. I took the food and a chuck wagon and met them at their campground. The kids bedrolled and camped—they had a great time. One night some of the parents drove out, because they thought their kids were having way too much fun, and were surprised to see that all of them were asleep. "Well, what do you expect?" Casey said. The kids had ridden fifteen to twenty miles! That was probably in the late sixties. When we didn't do campouts, I took the kids riding in the bosque along the river. It was all very rewarding.

Tony Hillerman was born in Sacred Heart, Oklahoma, in 1925 and has lived in Albuquerque for more than fifty years. An award-winning writer, he is the author of over twenty books, including fifteen in his Leaphorn and Chee series. His most recent book is Skeleton Man *(HarperCollins, 2005). A student of southwestern history and culture, Hillerman often draws his themes from the conflict between modern society and traditional Native American values and customs. He has received Edgar and Grand Master awards from the Mystery Writers of America and the 2002 Lifetime Achievement Award from Malice Domestic. His autobiography,* Seldom Disappointed *(HarperCollins, 2001), won the Agatha Award for best nonfiction from Malice Domestic. The Albuquerque Museum Foundation honored him as a Notable New Mexican in 2004. He received a master's degree from the University of New Mexico, where he taught for twenty years.*

Tony Hillerman

The first day I saw Albuquerque was in 1945. I was in a truck caravan from Oklahoma City with oil field equipment. I was in the army on a sixty-day convalescent furlough. Though when I read my papers, it said "thirty days." So I took a pen and turned it to "sixty." I was just back from Europe from the hospital. I got to Albuquerque on old Route 66 and went up Nine Mile Hill. I was dropped off at Crownpoint. It was my first experience with Navajos, and I went to a curing ceremony. I had one patch over an eye and was in my uniform, and I was on my way back to Albuquerque. Anyone could hitchhike then and especially when you were wearing a uniform. I got to Nine Mile Hill and looked down on Albuquerque, then about 45,000 people, and I remember the lights. I went to the main library, and I was impressed with how friendly everyone was, with the blue skies and clean air.

It took a while to get back. The next coming back was when my wife, Marie, and I moved to Santa Fe in 1950. I was editor of the *New*

Mexican, and I wanted to write a novel. Marie urged me to. By 1954 I had gotten feelers from the University of New Mexico and was offered a part-time job by Tom Popejoy [UNM president in the late fifties and early sixties], and I could work on my master's as well. We had four or five kids then, and Marie told me to do it, that we'd make out all right. So I became acquainted with the ivory tower of academia . . . it's a

A Suitable Place for Writing
While his books take place elsewhere in New Mexico, Tony Hillerman finds comfort in Albuquerque as a place to live and work. Courtesy Tony Hillerman, 2005.

mystical world. My job with Popejoy was doing undignified deeds, and no one knew what I did! Well, Popejoy lined up a grant to get the medical school going, but the bill we had to get passed was hung up. "We can't afford a medical school," the senators said. So Popejoy called me and said the sheriff of Bernalillo County would call. He did and told me, "We had a fire here at the jail. The boys burned up all the mattresses. I thought the university might have some spare mattresses." He needed about thirteen. The football stadium was in the middle of campus then, and we had a big Peace Corps camp set up. I told him, "I can give you your mattresses." So I did. One of the senators was the sheriff's brother, and he said, "I owe you. What can I do for you? You're looking for money for the med school, right?" So he changed the vote from a "no" to a "yes."

Another time had to do with Quito, Ecuador. The university had a study of cosmic rays down there. We had three students in jail. Tom Popejoy said to me, "I want you to take this package down there. So my wife and I went. Everyone wondered what I was doing down there because I was not a physicist and couldn't speak Spanish, but I got the students out of jail. That bag was probably full of money!

This city is a crossroads town and always has been. It's a mixture of wanderers coming through and stopping. There are the beautiful skies and migratory paths of birds. We have the sandhill cranes and piñon jays. The coyotes come trotting down the ditch and are very polite here. They will step aside to let you go by, unlike the Rottweilers.

If I could single out one thing that makes Albuquerque so nice, it would be these ditches—they allow people to walk up and down them. Mostly, there's not much action from Albuquerque that goes into my books, but it is a wonderful place to write.

Practical Place
*The city has offered artist
Florence Pierce a place to
create and raise a family.
Her paintings of lumi-
nous color stem from her
studies with Taos painter
Emil Bisttram. Courtesy
Charlotte Jackson
Gallery, Santa Fe.*

*Florence Pierce was born in 1918 in Washington, D.C. At seventeen she
left home for Taos, where she studied at the Emil Bisttram School of Fine
Art and became the youngest member of the Transcendental Painting
Group, formed in 1938. Members were known for their abstract, nonob-
jective style of painting. Pierce was one of only two women in the group,
which also included her husband, Horace. Her paintings appear in public
and private collections around the country. She has lived in Albuquerque
for over fifty years.*

I've been in and out of Albuquerque since I was a child. My grandfather came here to teach at the University of New Mexico and then
started working as chief plant pathologist for the U.S. Forest Service.
My grandfather was Doc Long [a
popular picnic area in the Sandia
Mountains is named after him]. My
folks tried living here when I was
three, but my father missed Wash-

Florence Pierce

ington, D.C., so much that we went back. I remember frolicking in the mountain streams. Then my husband and I moved here in 1948 or 1949, after a detour through New York and Los Angeles.

We've had different lives here. We came for practical reasons—for work and to paint and raise a family. But my husband died not long after we got here. I stayed. I don't know where we [she and her son] would have gone. Now I would never leave. I used to have attachments to Taos, but I've gotten so I really like being in Albuquerque. I like the feel of the city, the museums.

My work is not inspired by my environment. I'm saying that and I hope I'm accurate! The mountains do something for me—I like them at night. I lie in my bedroom and look out at the stars and the mountains, but views don't matter at all when I'm working, just the space [her studio]. There's no distraction there because it is made to work in. I have two rooms. One is where I do the resin work [which gives her paintings a luminous glow], and the other is where I do my drawing and hang my work. I'd rather work than anything else. I like keeping to myself.

Joe Powdrell moved to Albuquerque from Texas when he was young and has lived in Albuquerque for over forty years. He and his father own and manage Powdrell's Barbecue. He went through junior high and high school in Albuquerque and graduated from the University of New Mexico on a track-and-field scholarship. Powdrell earned his master's degree from the University of California, Fresno, in public administration. He served in Vietnam and is president of the Albuquerque chapter of the National Association for the Advancement of Colored People.

We had family here as early as the late 1930s. My dad had an uncle and two cousins. Our family migrated westward from Louisiana to East Texas to West Texas—that's where I was born—to New Mexico, and there are those who have gone on to the far West Coast. We came in pursuit of opportunity—everything this democracy offers, social justice. When I was about twelve [in 1958], we moved here. When you ask what was most pronounced or what stands out to me, it's clear to me now . . . but it wasn't clear to me then. Regard for your humanity was different. We here in Albuquerque had to grow, to learn how to regard others in an integrated society. We're almost there, but we still grapple with it some, and that's the end of that story!

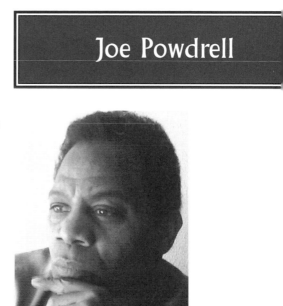

Joe Powdrell

I went to school in what Albuquerque would call the South Broad-

Barbecue Business

Joe Powdrell and his family have served their authentic smokey barbecue at the State Fair, weddings, divorces, and political rallies for decades. "We've seen a lot happen in this community. We've even watched dogs graduate from obedience class."

way and South Valley area: "South San Jose." It was mainly made up of blacks and Hispanics. There was a family there that had come from Mississippi, and their place was where people started—we were in their small house. There were eleven kids in my family, and it was a confined space.

Back in Odessa, Texas, Mom and Dad lived in a partitioned tent in '44, where one side was living quarters and the other a restaurant . . . so they've always had barbecue places. My dad's grandfather had given him a recipe for sauce and barbecue, and he used that. Here, they opened a place on South Broadway in 1962. It lasted five months. Dad was working on the other side of the mountains for Valley Gold Dairy. He was hauling hay provided by Bruce King. They got to be good friends and still are. He did construction for Bob Stamm, and they became good friends. They still get together and laugh.

In 1969 we started a restaurant again. I attribute our success to the cultural and societal wave in this country. It was the Age of Aquarius—do you know what I mean? We went from making barbecue sauce out of a pot to using fifty-gallon vats. All along we would tell ourselves, "Be honest, put out a good product consistently and joyfully. Be content! After all, look at where you've come from."

The restaurant business has been a challenge—some family members have gone to find different forms of work. Oh, but the things we've been a part of here—you can't put a value on it—all the way from funerals to births and everything in between. The political things, the cultural things, the weddings, the divorces; people graduating from college in their seventies. We've been on the ground floor of the Balloon Fiesta and catered that from its beginnings. We've been at the fair. We fed ten thousand people at a political party, where the winner wanted to say thank you to the people. We've met some prominent people in the process—Billy Graham, Bill Cosby, Martin Luther King's daughter, Malcolm X's daughter, Spike Lee, Danny Glover, Muhammad Ali. All this depends on how you regard your experience . . . for me, I'm rich in experience.

Carnis Salisbury was born in Caldwell, Texas, on January 1, 1914. She received her undergraduate degree from Wiley College and her master's from Gammon Theological Seminary. She was dean of women at Sam Houston College and worked for the federal government from 1947 to 1981. She was state president of the National Association for the Advancement of Colored People and a member of the New Mexico Civil Rights Advisory Committee to the U.S. Civil Rights Commission and is active in the National Council of Negro Women. Her honors include the Albuquerque Living Treasure Award, New Mexico Distinguished Public Service Award, Distinguished Woman of New Mexico Award, and Albuquerque Human Rights Award, which she won in recognition of getting the 1963 Fair Housing Ordinance passed.

Race Relations
Carnis Salisbury believes helping people learn to live together is her moral responsibility. "I've got to do it for my survival," she said. "All you have to do is reach out." Courtesy Carnis Salisbury.

My husband, Oliver Salisbury, and I came to Albuquerque in 1960. We came from Washington, D.C. My husband was in his middle age and had a hard time breathing . . . he had

Carnis Salisbury

asthma. We got in the car and started driving, and his breathing got better as we got away from moisture. He stayed in the veteran's hospital for a year. I knew I needed to be here with him, so the State Department said, "You go and we'll help you find a job with the government." I was a research clerk working on Taiwan and Southeast Asia, and my husband worked on Russia, translating Russian documents. We loved Washington and our jobs, but we had to go.

Well, finding a job in the government was no small task. Back in the sixties, there were not a lot of jobs just waiting for someone to take. I went down a level, but it was worth it. Finally, when my husband was about to leave the hospital, a man came looking for him. He hired him to work in staff development for the state welfare department. Our two girls were still in Washington . . . one was sixteen or seventeen, and the youngest was in the third grade. I had to send for them and find a house. Looking for a home in the 1960s was quite an assignment. This is the friendliest place that I've ever lived in. But when it came to finding a job or a house, I got, "Oh, we can't sell our house to you. Our neighbors wouldn't like that." But when you have a sick husband and two daughters, there's no choice. We met a man who worked for the university who wanted to sell us his house, but he had to get permission from the Board of Regents. He finally sold us his home.

I took to living in my community [they were the only black family in the Southeast Heights] as a project. We were very cautious about things we did. I wanted our house to look good, with fresh paint. I was determined I would take it all [any prejudice] in stride. I told myself, "If this is a project, I won't let it get under my skin." My father told us you don't make decisions when you are in a fever. So I tried to pick up whatever leads I could find to help me be an ideal person in our neighborhood. At first our neighbors put newspaper and curtains in their garage windows so we couldn't see each other. But little by little, neighbors would talk to us across the fence . . . I had the feeling I was among friends. We lived there for thirty-five years. I still go back to visit.

My first job was at Sandia Base. I'd never been on a job I hated before—counting nuts and bolts. I loved the people, but the job I couldn't stand! A man from the National Association for the Advancement of Colored People came to see us and said there were a lot of government agencies without blacks. That's how I got my next job, with the IRS—when this man pointed out to them that they hadn't hired any black people. People are strange, and I don't think they realized how prejudiced that was. That was Albuquerque then. The town was small.

I found that I was not the only person interested in better race relations. All I had to do was reach out. My husband's and my big project was getting the Fair Housing Ordinance passed. In the sixties, there was a commission of three people that governed the city's housing department. We had a big meeting, and all the real estate agents, contractors, and developers showed up and said, "We don't need this ordinance." Well, my husband stood up and told those people that Albuquerque had a problem, and a serious problem, and then told them about our experience. When he was finished, the commissioners said, "We're passing the Fair Housing Ordinance now." And they did. That was our greatest achievement. We wanted our children not to have to go through what we went through to get a house. It doesn't mean all problems have been solved, but we feel we have found many people equally interested in fair housing and fair employment.

Since then, my work has been with organizations that are interested in civil rights. At first, I had a hard time getting announcements and news of what we did in the paper. Then I met Concha Ortiz y Pino de Klevin [well known for her work in civil and women's rights]. She said, "I'll tell you how to get in the paper if you teach me how to make cornbread!" We've been friends ever since.

Lights, Action . . . Fusion
In efforts to create a powerful form of energy, scientists test the Z machine at Sandia Laboratories. Photograph by Randy Montoya. Courtesy Sandia National Laboratories, 2004.

From Thin Air

High Tech, Flying Balloons, and South Valley Magic

Patty Anderson came to Albuquerque from North Dakota, where she attended the University of North Dakota and married Maxie Anderson. She spends the majority of her time supporting hot-air ballooning efforts and has been integral in creating the Anderson-Abruzzo Albuquerque International Balloon Museum, of which she is board chair. She has served on the board of the St. Joseph Hospital Foundation and helped in many of its fund-raising events. Her family owns and runs a vineyard in the North Valley.

Patty Anderson

Maxie and I came to Albuquerque with our three children from the University of North Dakota in the late 1950s. The uranium mining business was booming at the time. Max was in engineering and got really interested in mining, and he talked his dad into uranium prospects in Grants. [His business became Ranchers Exploration and Development Corporation.]

We bought probably one of the first balloons in town from Sid Cutter. He wanted a balloon, and it was his mother's birthday. So he had a big party for her out at his hangar at the Albuquerque Airport. Of course, she had no interest in the balloon at all! So Sid started flying it. Soon after, Max got in with Sid, and they got up in the air and flew around a little bit. They were both new pilots. When they landed, Sid asked, "Do you want to fly, Max?" Max said, "Sure." So Sid got out of the basket, and off went Max by himself. That's how he started flying! There wasn't much in the way of certification or anything back then. It was just by the seat of your pants. That's how I learned, too. We didn't realize you aren't supposed to take off in winds more than ten miles per hour, so we had some wild takeoffs and landings. It became a family sport for us. We took the kids with us and had them help us launch the balloon. We went to balloon races. Kris [their son] has set a number of records. He flew with Maxie on the *Kitty Hawk* in the first transcontinental crossing [in 1980].

Transatlantic Crossing
The city celebrates returning ballonists Maxie Anderson, Ben Abuzzo,
and Larry Newman in 1978. Courtesy Patty Anderson.

In the first Balloon Fiesta [in 1973], there were thirteen pilots . . .
and I think Sid flew our balloon in that one. Then Maxie flew in the
second fiesta, when it was at the fairgrounds. It was February and it
snowed on him. I remember when he went up, I couldn't see him, and
he disappeared in the snow. Now, this city is a big ballooning city.
There are a lot of hot-air balloonists who love ballooning, and the Balloon Fiesta is the big event of the year.

The effort to start the museum [the Anderson-Abruzzo Albuquerque International Balloon Museum] didn't start until after Max
was gone. [He died in a ballooning accident in 1983, along with fellow
balloonist and Albuquerquean Don Ida.] My son Mike and I started
thinking about starting a museum in 1984, and now twenty years later
we're seeing the culmination of our work. We went to the state legislature to get funding. We went to City Hall, to the City Commission
meetings. It was a long process and not an easy process. Now, with the
help of private donations and city funding, we have a huge building—
60,000 square feet—at Fiesta Park, which opened in September 2005.

It has classrooms, educational programs, a library with one of the largest collections of books, periodicals, and pictures of the history of ballooning and of flight in general. We have the Fugo bomb, the bomb the Japanese floated in a hot-air balloon into the western United States and Canada during World War II. One section is devoted to military balloons. We have the envelope that a lady made out of sheets, and her family flew with it over the Iron Curtain to escape. We have a harness trapeze that was used during the barnstorming days, when the husband flew in the basket and the gal did trapeze acts while hanging underneath.

We've been collecting things for twenty years, and when people saw this was a reality, the donations started coming in from all over the world. We're doing a replica of the *Double Eagle II* [Maxie, Ben Abruzzo, and Larry Newman flew it in the first transatlantic crossing in 1978, a benchmark in ballooning history] because the Smithsonian won't release ours. This museum will be amazing.

Donald Cook came to Albuquerque in 1977, when he was twenty-nine, as a graduate of Massachusetts Institute of Technology. He had received his undergraduate degree from the University of Michigan. He is director of Sandia National Laboratories' MESA Program Center and has directed the labs' Pulsed Power Sciences Center and managed its Fusion Research Department. He enjoys riding motorcycles, running, and skiing.

Albuquerque's April nights. They are perfect nights when you can see the peaks and different parts of the mountains . . . they really do turn purplish, and if you are paying attention to where you are and the sun is at its final stage of setting, the mountains are just beautiful. And you can see real stars. These nights, the work at the labs, and this crazy guy named Gerry Yonas [a principal scientist and vice president of Sandia Labs] are what attracted me to come here. Yonas talked about making energy with fusion. It's based upon the power of the stars, and it works on a big scale—whenever a pressure is large, the density of matter and the temperature get high. Then there is a fusion reaction that starts to produce energy. Although not limitless, the stars have burned [by fusion] for millions and millions

Donald Cook

of years. The Greeks used to dream of having the power of the sun on earth, and Gerry Yonas was talking about actually doing that. I worked in this area from 1977 to 1999. I've worked with exceptional people.

Time and Thought
Donald Cook says his thinking is clearest when he rides his motorcycle along New Mexico's scenic drives. Photograph by Randy Montoya. Courtesy Sandia National Laboratories, 2005.

We're not there yet, but we've come a long way toward making fusion work as a source of energy. We've built the Z machine, the most powerful X-ray-producing machine on the planet. [The X-rays compress energy in rapid pulses to create fusion.] Fusion is the source of sunlight and is the cleanest supply of energy mankind has found. With the Z machine, we started with hopes and dreams, and now we have real plans.

Since 1999 I've led the team in building our micro-systems facility. With MESA [Microsystems and Engineering Sciences Application], we're trying to do for the world what no one else has. It's micro everything—micro-electronics, micro-machines, micro-optics, and micro-photonics, or lasers. We're working on one-billionth of a meter—on that level—for computers, TV sets, cell phones, telecommunications systems, cameras, MP3 players, the whole field of commercial electronics. [MESA also is working on modernizing the safety and security of the country's weapons stockpile.]

While at work, I go in my car to the edge of our site and sit and think. I do my best thinking in my car, looking out at a New Mexico landscape and drinking a diet soda. It's amazing how much I can accomplish out there! It's a way to release stress. "Get out! Free your mind!" I tell all my employees. The beauty of New Mexico is that you can get out of the fray. The natural beauty opens the mind and the spirit.

I love speed, whether it's driving a motorcycle or working with the Z machine or micro-electronics. So in work I ask, "How fast is fast?" and apply the question to the physics of fusion. And in my personal life, well, there's nothing like driving a motorcycle. I have four. I have one that my wife rides with me—it goes a little slower than the others. One of my two favorite rides is to go from Albuquerque on Fourth Street all the way up to Bernalillo, then north through San Ysidro, by the cliffs and flowing streams, past Valle Grande to Los Alamos, Santa Fe, and down through Madrid on Highway 14, and back home. The other ride is south through Chilili, Torreon, Mountainair, and Los Lunas, then back. On the northern ride, I've done it in four hours—well I've done it faster, but I'm not saying how fast.

Miguel Gandert was born in Espanola in 1956, grew up in Santa Fe, and lived in South America before moving to Albuquerque in 1972 to become a student at the University of New Mexico. He worked at Channel 7 for more than fourteen years and has been a professor in the Communications Department at the University of New Mexico since 1991. He now occupies the same office as that of his favorite professor, Tony Hillerman. Gandert's photographs appear in his book Nuevo México Profundo: Rituals of an Indo-Hispano Homeland *(MNM Press) and in public collections such as the Smithsonian's National Museum of American History; the Center for Creative Photography in Tucson, Arizona; the Beinke Rare Book and Manuscript Library at Yale; and the New Mexico Museum of Fine Arts.*

I have a photograph of Andre the Giant, a wrestler who became a movie star, and I photographed him with Mike London, the big wrestling promoter, at the Civic Auditorium. To me, Andre's a historic figure. Growing up in New Mexico, living in Albuquerque, every Sunday you watched championship wrestling with fake lockers that were brought in and shot in the studio at Channel 7. White port, muscatel, and sherry sponsored this show . . . I had no idea what those were when I was a little kid. Then, when I was twenty, here I was photographing Mike London and Andre the Giant at the Civic Auditorium!

Miguel Gandert

I did a whole series of photographs called Two Corners of a Ring. It was pictures of boxing gyms in South Broadway and theatrical championship wrestling at the Civic Auditorium. I have pictures of what was inside the Civic Auditorium: Roller Derby, wrestling, rock concerts. Roller Derby was unbelievable—I was there watching that.

What's so great about Albuquerque is that it's made up of a lot of villages or communities. I have been intrigued with so many stories constantly evolving, and the South Valley is where I've spent hours and hours. It's the core of my work. When I walked out of the boxing

The Mystery before the Lens
Andre the Giant stands with promoter Mike London during Sunday-night wrestling at Civic Auditorium. 1975. Photograph by Miguel Gandert.

gym, I started photographing the community—Matachines dancing. And there's a sacred tortilla. People would go to pray where it was made. It hangs between Plexiglas with an image of Jesus on it. This is serious stuff! This is a place where magical things happen. Out of that community, I learned. It taught me how to look at people, to pay attention to detail . . . to find their humanity. I had to learn to respect them. There was one Hispanic youth who wanted his picture taken with his gun. I told him he had to put it away, that I wouldn't photograph him with it. So he did, and after a while I knew this kid was here to teach me something. I came away with some shots of the guy, his nature, yet he was able to keep his dignity.

A lot of the mysteries of Albuquerque have come in front of my camera. Just recently I photographed this suspension ritual that kids are doing now, just four hundred yards from this university. People hang from hooks that are pierced through the skin. It was amazing. With the camera you can go anywhere—that's the joy of being a photographer.

Neighborhoods and landmarks are fondly

recalled in the reflections of Albuquerque natives, but not one person failed to express chagrin at the city's growth and the challenge of driving across town. As with many cities, such as Salt Lake City, Raleigh, Chicago, or Denver, Albuquerque's downtown has languished since the 1970s because people have moved to outlying neighborhoods. The ties that bind people to downtown have weakened. And like these other cities, where mayors and city planners are trying to pull citizens back to their cities' cores, so, too, are Albuquerque strategists.

Coined the "New Urbanist" movement, the trend is to make downtown vital again, and in Albuquerque that involves creating a place where people across economic lines can live, work, shop, and relax as they once did when Albuquerque was but a village around a plaza. The planned

Epilogue
A City Revitalized

gathering spot will include a movie theatre housing fourteen screens, an underground parking lot, retail spaces, and once-neglected build-

opposite page top
A Ghostly Downtown
The call of new homes on large lots and new business buildings drew people away from downtown's closer quarters in the 1980s. Empty streets and vacant parking lots were a common sight. Photo by Dick Ruddy, 1982.

opposite page bottom
Changes in the Making
The First and Central intersection, the historical heart of Albuquerque's downtown, reflects attention and thought given to a higher volume of traffic. Revitalization projects such as the Alvarado Transportation Center, formerly the Alvarado Hotel on the far left, and the Century Fourteen Movie Theatre, just beyond the center in the photo, pull people back to the city's core. The Century Movie facility is where the old European Hotel was erected in 1880. Photo by Dick Ruddy, 2005.

A Morning Stroll in the Plaza

The Civic Plaza brings to downtown what the people behind the city's revitalization hope for: pedestrians, runners, bikers, and those gathering for break-times from work. City Hall is right of center and the Albuquerque/Bernalillo County office building is center. Photo by Dick Ruddy, 2005.

ings turned into lofts sold condominiums for work and residential uses. The community support behind this revitalization could make a believer out of those who have watched the city go through many tries at breathing life into its faltering downtown.

"Downtown Albuquerque is 'New Mexico's Downtown,'" states the Historic District Improvement Company, a partner in the changes afoot, noting that the city is the only true urban place in the entire state. City arts organizations promote the move downtown as artists throughout history have pioneered forgotten neighborhoods and helped attract crowds to gallery openings, literary events, and performances. Cafés and restaurants popular in other parts of the city are beginning to open for business in renovated buildings. A walk down Central on a weekday confirms that this is a downtown on the move. People are busily crisscrossing the city streets, and cars are parked overtime on flashing meters. On the downtown fringe, the convention center isn't yet fully booked. It's huge hollow space lies dormant much of the time. But with over $400 million allocated toward revitalization, the sense is that this spot, too, will have its bright future.

One of the partners rooted in the revitalization effort is Owen Lopez, executive director of the McCune Charitable Foundation in Santa Fe, a philanthropic organization established in 1989 by the McCune family.

Owen Lopez

I was born in 1941 in Albuquerque and raised there. I went to St. Mary's School through the tenth grade, then I went away to boarding school and on to law school. My grandfather, Owen Marron, was First Assistant Superintendent of the Indian School in Albuquerque in 1888 and was mayor of Albuquerque in 1900 and 1901. He became the first Treasurer of State in 1912. His wife, my grandmother, Frances Halloran, was born in

Albuquerque in 1880 and was a regent at the University of New Mexico. Marron Hall at the university was named after my grandmother. My dad came from New Jersey in 1935. You'd think the Lopezes would be the old ones, but go figure! When I was born, Albuquerque was a town of 40,000. I walked and rode my bike to school. We lived near the country club area…there were not too many people named Lopez around there. I had a paper route in Barelas. Being raised as what we used to call a "coyote," or half Anglo and half Hispano, always made it a challenge. There was certain distaste from the country club crowd, and in the barrio (a reference to Barrelas) we weren't really welcome either. It made my siblings and I pretty tolerant. We learned to cut deep to the truth about classes and discrimination.

Back then Albuquerque was a frumpy little town. We didn't have a key to our house because no one locked anything. We went to the movies on Saturdays. We saw *King Kong* at the KiMo and *Giant* at the Sunshine. The State Fair was a big event then, and I remember the rope tow up at Sandia Ski Area where I learned to ski. I went away to school from 1957 to 1968; the changes in the city during that period were dramatic. I came back from law school and settled in Santa Fe, where I was a natural resource lawyer dealing with mining and the gas industry in the state for twenty five years. When I came to the McCune Foundation in 1993 I got involved in social issues. It astonished me at what little thought went into Albuquerque's planning and development. In Old Town and downtown, there once was a sense of community, then came the university and Nob Hill and people moved there, then came the 1970s when people moved further away and downtown died. I gave my father a hard time by asking him, "What were you country-club-types doing?" He just said he was paying more attention to making a living to support our family than to planning how the city grew.

My mother is still living in the house where I grew up. My siblings still live in Albuquerque. So we've all stuck around! But the problem facing the city and state today is keeping our college graduates here. We need to create jobs so people can and want to live here.

Now, the McCune Foundation is interested in social issues. Six years ago, we came together with Jim Baca, former Albuquerque mayor; Pat Bryan of the Historic District Improvement Company (HDIC); and Christopher Leinberger, also of HDIC [a nationally recognized strategist behind the country's new urban development projects] and together we are committed to investing in Albuquerque's downtown. Since we've been working together, we've seen a remarkable turnaround. I attribute that to our private-public relationship. This is a "patient" investment where we are not looking for a fast return and there is interest in a social good where we can provide affordable housing. At McCune, our philanthropy solely wasn't going to gain much traction, but with private money combined we are seeing change. The Century Theatre Block is fully developed along with the Gold Street Lofts—[a structure for retail, art galleries, restaurants, and residential lofts sold as condominiums]. This is the area between First and Third, which includes the historic First and Central intersection. There seems to be a pent-up demand for urban living, and I think we are offering people that now.

My hopes are that in working in Albuquerque we can bridge the divide between it and Santa Fe. It's silly what we two cities do. We can help one another through art and cultural programs. For instance, the KiMo and the Lensic, both historic theaters, can work together in programming performing arts and visual arts events. We could see better coordination. I'm hopeful that the next generation will rise to the occasion.

I want to see downtown become a residential place for middle- to low-income families and a place where these people can work. It can become a center for commerce and industry where you can walk. Downtown Chicago and Portland, Oregon, are amazing, for these cities have created such an atmosphere. That's what Albuquerque can be.